Go

The Spirit in the World

by

Donald L. Gelpi, S.J.

Michael Glazier
Wilmington, Delaware

About the Author

Donald L. Gelpi, S.J., is currently on the theology faculty at the Jesuit School of Theology at Berkeley, California. Among his publications are *The Divine Mother: A Trinitarian Theology of the Holy Spirit* and *Experiencing God: A Theology of Human Emergence*, and he has also contributed extensively to scholarly journals in the theological field.

Library of Congress Catalog Card Number: 88-82454
International Standard Book Numbers:
Zacchaeus Studies, Theology: 0-89453-680-X
GOD BREATHES: THE SPIRIT IN THE WORLD: 0-89453-684-2

Cover Design by Maureen Daney
Typography by Phyllis LaVane
Printed in the United States of America. SM

TABLE OF CONTENTS

Editor's Note on Zacchaeus Studies

This series of short texts in doctrinal subjects is designed to offer introductory volumes accessible to any educated reader. Dealing with the central topics of Christian faith, the authors have set out to explain the theological interpretation of these topics in a Catholic context without assuming a professional theological training on the part of the reader.

We who have worked on the series hope that these books will serve well in college theology classes where they can be used either as a series or as individual introductory presentations leading to a deeper exploration of a particular topic. We also hope that these books will be widely used and useful in adult study circles, continuing education and RENEW programs, and will be picked up by casual browsers in bookstores. We want to serve the needs of any who are trying to understand more thoroughly the meaning of the Catholic faith and its relevance to the changing circumstances of our times.

Each author has endeavored to present the biblical foundation, the traditional development, the official church position and the contemporary theological discussion of the doctrine or topic in hand. Controversial questions are discussed within the context of the established teaching and the accepted theological interpretation.

We undertook the series in response to increasing interest among educated Catholics in issues arising in the contemporary church, doctrines that raise new questions in a contemporary setting, and teachings that now call for wider and deeper appreciation. To such people we offer these volumes, hoping that reading them may be a satisfying and heartening experience.

Monika K. Hellwig
Series Editor

1

God Breathes on Israel

Most people think of Death Valley as a barren, forbidding place, hostile to human survival; but in the spring Death Valley comes alive with wild flowers. The eye expands before seemingly endless vistas, gazing through the balmy, crystalline air as the sun in its passage etches each crevasse of the Panamint and Grapevine ranges.

One spring I visited the Valley with a group of friends. On the third day the winds struck us. In the spring flash floods pose no threat to Death Valley campers; but high winds can swoop down without warning. They sweep across the salt flats scouring the alluvial fans at the base of the mountains. A haze hangs in the air not of moisture but of minute dust particles.

Once they start blowing, the winds can persist. They whistled around us for three days. The members of our party tried to ignore them the first day. After two days of steady gusting, we showed signs of uneasiness. By the third day, the ceaseless gale had begun to give us the willies. We decided to leave a day before we had planned.

A contemporary scientist might have tried to explain our early departure by suggesting that the high number of positive ions in dry desert winds can make people jittery and even ill. The ancient Hebrews would, however, have described our reactions to the wind very differently. They would have said that we had felt God breathing.

The term "spirit" meant something very different to the people who wrote the Old Testament from what it means to people today. When contemporary Christians hear the term "spirit" they tend to oppose it to the term "matter." We think of a spirit as something incorporeal, ethereal, insubstantial.

In contemporary versions of the Bible, the English word "spirit" translates the Hebrew word *ruah.* In the Hebrew Bible, however, the term *ruah* does not signify something incorporeal, ethereal, or unsubstantial. It means wind in motion, active breathing. Moreover, for the ancient Hebrews breath meant life. Living people breathe, the dead breathe no more. When, therefore, the ancient Hebrews spoke of the *ruah,* or Breath of God, they imagined a life force as powerful, uncanny, and uncontrollable as a desert sirocco. They imagined, in other words, something like the howling winds that swept down unexpectedly on us in Death Valley.

In the course of this book we are going to try to take a fresh look at an old Christian belief. We are going to reexamine what Christians mean when they say that they believe in the Holy Spirit. Sometimes, however, familiar terms can stand in the way of seeing familiar realities with new eyes. Because the familiar term "spirit" means for us something very different from what it meant to the authors of the Bible, it could betray us all too easily into misunderstanding the Hebrew term *ruah.* Let me then suggest that we replace "spirit," the usual English translation of *ruah,* with a less familiar image. Let us translate *ruah* as "breath," and let us speak not of the Holy Spirit but of the Holy Breath of God. Every time you see the new term, let it remind you, then, that in the Bible the term "spirit" does not mean something abstract, ethereal, or insubstantial. On the contrary, in the pages of the Bible the Holy Breath of God acts with a power that resembles the physical force of the wind.

As confessing Christians we should not, however, imagine the Holy Breath of God as an impersonal force but as a personal, empowering, life-giving presence. The very suggestion that we should call a divine person "the Breath of God" suggests, then, another linguistic and imaginative problem connected with the third person of the trinity: namely, that even though the Christian creed confesses three persons in one God, Christians lack personal names and images for the third member of the divine triad.

As we shall see, both Scripture and tradition sanction imagining the third person of the trinity as the feminine face of God; and in recent years the idea has been gaining more general theological acceptance. Since, then, we hope to take a new look at the Holy Breath of God, let us adopt another new linguistic convention for talking about the third person of the trinity. Besides calling her the Holy Breath, I shall in the pages that follow also refer to her with a feminine pronoun.

The overall argument of this book divides into five chapters. The present chapter reflects on the ways in which God breathed upon Israel before the coming of Jesus. Chapter two examines how God's Holy Breath inspired Jesus' life and mission. Chapter three ponders her action in the church. Chapter four probes her presence in the world at large. Chapter five meditates on the divine Breath's personal reality and discovers in her the feminine face of God.

This first chapter, then, focuses on the divine Breath's action in the Old Testament. First, it examines the link made in the Hebrew Bible between life and breath, on the one hand, and the saving action of God's Holy Breath, on the other. The second section of this chapter explores the witness of the Hebrew prophets to the Breath's inspirations. Section three meditates what the wise men of Israel wrote about the divine Breath's activity and reality. Section four describes her inspiration of the great leaders of Israel and the growth of messianic hope among the Jews. The final section of this chapter ponders the challenges to contemporary faith which the Old Testament witness to the divine Breath's saving action poses.

I. The Breath of Life and God's Breathing.

The second chapter of Genesis links the concept of life and the image of breath clearly and unmistakably. God forms Adam's body from clay and breathes into his nostrils the breath of life (Gen 2:4b, 7). Adam alone receives the breath of life directly from the lips of God. Adam therefore rises from the earth constrained to cling to the God of life or suffer the deadly consequences of sin (Gen 2:16-17).

After Adam and Eve sin, God not only bars them from the tree of life but also decrees that no human shall live more than one hundred and twenty years (Gen 6:32; Wis 15:11). With death the human breath of life returns to the God who gave it; and no created power can command its return (Ps 31:6; Wis 11:26-12:1, 16:14).

Having turned from God to sin, humankind lives powerless in the face of its own death-bound, sinful state. Only God can undo the deadly effects of sin; and he does so through the action of his holy, life-giving Breath. The earliest historical texts in the Old Testament link the divine Breath's action to an empowering religious enlightenment. God breathes upon prophets like Balaam in order that the prophet may declare to God's chosen people his saving intentions (Num 24:2).

The Holy Breath, however, imparts other kinds of religious enlightenment besides prophetic inspiration. She inspires religious wisdom (Gen 41:38), prayer (Zech 12:10), artistic creativity (Ex 31:3ff). In moments of crisis, the divine Breath raises up inspired leaders like Moses, Joshua, and the Judges (Num 11:17-30, Judg 3:10, 11:29, 13:25, 14:6-19).

The Breath of God inspires holy enlightenment in those on whom she descends: faith, covenant fidelity, sensitivity to God's saving acts. The Hebrews recognized, however, that not every impulse which humans experience proceeds from God. When, for example. Saul, the first king of Israel, disobeyed God's command and sinned, a breath of evil descended upon him plunging him into dark and violent moods (1 Sam 15:1-31, 16:14-23). Saul learned the hard way that an evil breath brings darkness of spirit, violence of heart, hypocrisy, and deceit. It blinds one to God's saving activity (Is 29:10).

II. The Breath of Prophecy.

In speaking of prophetic inspiration we need to distinguish between ecstatic and classical prophecy. The classical prophets wrote down their oracles, which were collected and preserved in the prophetic books of the Old Testament. Because they wrote down their religious inspirations, often in sublime poetry, scholars sometimes call the classical prophets writing prophets.

Because we possess the writings of the classical prophets, we know first hand about the way they perceived religious realities. Viewed historically, however, the ecstatic prophets came first. The ecstatic prophets left behind no writings, but we can reconstruct something about their careers from some of the historical books of the Old Testament: Joshua and Judges, the first and second books of Samuel, and the first and second books of Kings.

The ecstatic prophets seem to have uttered their oracles in a state of rapture that at times approached delirium or even frenzy. Sometimes groups of prophets proclaimed the word of God together and accompanied their prophecy with song and dance. When God breathed on the ecstatic prophet, the historical books of the Old Testament sometimes employ abrupt or even violent images to describe the event. The prophetic Breath rushed upon the prophet, seized hold of him. The violence of the descriptive language underscores the receptive stance of the prophet before the Breath's enlightenment (1 Sam 10:5-6, 19:18-24.)

The ecstatic prophets lived in religious communities. The Old Testament names Jericho (2 Kings 2:5-7), Gibeah (1 Sam 10:10), Rama (2 Kings 2:5-7), Gilgal (2 Kings 4:38), and other cities as centers of ecstatic prophecy. These prophetic communities cultivated distinctive dress and hair style (1

Kings 20:35ff, 2 Kings 1:8), shared a common table (1 Kings 22:1-6, 2 Kings 4:38–44), lived on alms and probably in poverty (Num 22:7, 2 Kings 6:5), were guided by a leader (1 Kings 20:35ff, 2 Kings 2:9), and probably lived in a cluster of cells or houses. Some had families (2 Kings 4:1ff, 1 Sam 8:1-5), others lived celibate lives (1 Kings 17, 2 Kings 18).

The writing prophets changed the style of Old Testament prophecy. Although some of them certainly had disciples, in contrast to the ecstatic prophets who lived in communities, the writing prophets confront us as distinctively individual religious voices. They proclaimed a personalized religious vision. Moreover, the tone of the message they announced savored of the secular. The classical prophets tackled the serious social, political, an cultic problems of their day with words of critical challenge and of hope. They addressed a stinging rebuke to the consciences of their contemporaries, denouncing moral depravity, human exploitation for political or economic motives, and the hypocrisy of worship that proceeds from unregenerate hearts. They cried out for social, political, and religious reform and for fidelity to the moral demands of Israel's covenant with God.

We find classical, or writing, prophets functioning at three important periods in the history of Israel. The pre-exilic prophets proclaimed God's word to the kingdoms of Israel and of Judah roughly from the middle of the eighth century before Christ until the capture of Jerusalem by the Babylonians in 587 B.C. During the period of the Babylonian exile, from 587 to 538 B.C., the exilic prophets preached a message of encouragement to the Jewish exiles and laid the foundations for the restoration of Judaism in the post-exilic period. For a brief time after the exile we find evidence of prophetic preaching, but by the end of the fourth century B.C., the prophetic voice had died in Israel. It would not sound again until John the Baptist emerged from the Judean deserts proclaiming a message of repentance for the forgiveness of sins.

During each of these three periods prophetic preaching made important contributions to the Hebrew understanding of the reality of God's holy Breath and of her role in salvation history. Let us glean those insights from each era of prophetic teaching beginning with the pre-exilic prophets.

The Pre-Exilic Prophets.

As we have just seen the historical books of the Old Testament all portray the ecstatic prophets as Breath-inspired. It comes, then, as some surprise that most of the pre-exilic writing prophets refused to own her as the source of their inspiration. They claimed instead inspiration by the word of God rather than by his Breath. Two pre-exilic prophets provided an exception to this pattern. Hosea conceded the derisive title his enemies used to ridicule him: they called him a "man of the Breath," one who claims her as the source of his preaching (Hos 9:7b). Micah invoked her divine authority in his denunciation of the sins of God's people (Mic 3:8). The reluctance which the pre-exilic prophets showed to claim God's Breath as the inspiration of their teaching seems to have flowed from a desire to distinguish their own preaching from the ministry of the ecstatic prophets, who were certainly regarded as "men of the Breath."

Paradoxically, however, this very reluctance on the part of the writing prophets who taught prior to the exile produced a prodigious development in theological understanding of the divine Breath's role within the history of salvation; for instead of resting content to speak out of the religious consciousness which the divine Breath inspired, the pre-exilic prophets described in considerable detail what the holy Breath of God accomplishes within salvation history. To put the matter briefly, while the ecstatic prophets experienced directly God breathing on them and responded to it, the classical, or writing, prophets before the exile described what the divine Breath accomplishes.

Not every use of the wind imagery in the writings of the pre-exilic prophets refers, however, to divine activity. Sometimes the image of wind connotes empty vanity or tumult (Ho 8:7). When, however, the pre-exilic prophets described the saving action of God's Breath, they linked it consistently to the themes of judgment and of moral righteousness.

The prophet Micah claimed the divine Breath's authority to pronounce judgment on Israel's immortality (Mic 3:8). The prophet Hosea imagined Israel as chaff swept away by the wind of divine judgment (Hos 4:19). Isaiah too likened God's judgment to a wind that blows away the chaff from threshed grain. It purifies the people of their moral filth and prepares them to accept the salvation which God offers them (Is 22:4:40). Jeremiah, however, who prophesied in Jerusalem on the eve of its destruction by the Babylonians, warned his generation that the approaching winds of divine judgment would bring not salvation but retribution: "A hot wind from the bare heights in the desert toward the daughter of my people, not to winnow and cleanse, a wind too full for this comes from me. Now it is I who speak in judgment upon them" (Jer 4:11-12).

Among the pre-exilic prophets Isaiah linked the divine Breath's inspiration to righteous living. Isaiah promised that the Breath of judgment and of burning would purge away the moral filth of God's people (Is 4:2-6). He also foretold that, when the Breath of God would be poured out from on high, that "justice will dwell in the wilderness, and righteousness abide in the fruitful field. And the effect of righteousness will be peace, and the result of righteousness, quietness and trust forever" (Is 32:14-17).

The pre-exilic prophets saw that resistance to the divine Breath's sanctifying enlightenment transforms her into the instrument of divine judgment. Then her prophetic inspirations unmask the hypocrisy of false prophecy and false mysticism and judge the moral deviation which springs from lack of faith in God.

The Prophets of the Exile.

Two great prophetic voices proclaimed God's word to his people during the Babylonian exile: Ezekiel and an anonymous prophet whom scholars call second Isaiah because his writings comprise the second part of the book of Isaiah.

Unlike the pre-exilic prophets, Ezekiel acknowledged freely that the Breath of God inspired his prophecies (Ezek 3:12, 14; 8:3; 11:1: 37:1; 43:5). He also proclaimed the Breath's power to reanimate the entire nation of Israel. The exiles might feel arid, lifeless, scattered like the bones of a slain army, but the word of God would re-assemble the bones and clothe them with sinews and with flesh. Not, however, until the Breath of God had re-animated them would Israel stand once again in dignity like the living army it once was (Ezek 37:1-14). Ezekiel foresaw the day dawning which the pre-exilic prophets had foretold in vain: the day when the holy Breath would effect repentant purification and moral reform in the hearts of God's people. When that day dawned she would seal a new covenant between God and those whom he had chosen (Ezek 36:23-31).

Second Isaiah shared the same hope of Israel's moral re-consecration to God. In God's name he promised that God would pour his Breath out upon the descendants of those in exile.

> They shall spring up like grass amid waters, like willows by flowing streams. This one will say, "I am the Lord's," another will call himself by the name of Jacob, and another will write on his hand "The Lord's," and surname himself by the name of Israel" (Is 44:3-5).

The prophets of exile also introduced a novel perception of the divine Breath which the wise men of Israel would develop in the generations that followed the exile. In what did that novel perception consist? As we have seen, the Old Testament consistently associated the activity of the divine Breath with the dawning of human religious consciousness. In the writings of Ezekiel, however, we find a hint that God's own presence to the world is mediated by his Breath.

In Ezekiel's inaugural vision, in which God commissions

him to prophesy, God appears to the prophet in human form riding in something like a chariot whose wheels are moved by four cherubim. Ultimately, however, the holy Breath of God herself moves both the cherubim and the wheels of the chariot itself. The image suggests that in some mysterious manner (how remains obscure) God through the Breath's action moves across his creation and becomes present to it (Ezek 1:1-21).

One may extract a similar insight from a complex passage in the writings of second Isaiah which describes the exodus of the Jews from Egypt under Moses's leadership. The prophet assured an exiled people that God himself, no messenger or angel, had intervened long ago to rescue his people from bondage. That memory should inspire confidence even in the midst of exile that God's love remains steadfast. When during their desert wanderings the chosen people "grieved" the Breath of God by disobeying her inspirations, God "fought against" them only for a time and through his saving Breath brought them home to the land he had promised (Is 63:9-14). The prophecy poses serious problems of interpretation, but it seems to suggest that God himself becomes present to his people through the action of his Breath.

As we shall see, in the period following the exile, the wise men of Israel would deepen and expand these hints found in the writings of the prophets of exile. They would identify the reality of God's holy Breath with his saving wisdom. In other words, they would portray her as the source not only of human religious consciousness but of God's own self-awareness.

Post-Exilic Prophecy.

In the period following the exile, two prophets developed the teachings of the prophets of exile concerning the saving action of God's holy Breath: Joel and another anonymous prophet called Third Isaiah because his writings comprise the third and final section of the book of Isaiah.

Third Isaiah took up a theme present in the preaching of Ezekiel. The latter had promised that by the saving action of his holy Breath God would seal a new covenant with his people. Third Isaiah promised further in God's name that nothing would have the power to break this new covenant (Is 59:21).

Joel, for his part, foretold that God would pour out His saving Breath not only on Israel but on "all flesh." She would come to effect the salvation of all people, whether Jew or gentile, young or old, male or female. She would transform the entire human race into God's prophetic people (Joel 3:1-5). On Pentecost day the apostle Peter would see in the arrival of the Holy Breath of Christ the fulfillment of Joel's prophecy (Acts 2:17-21).

III. God's Breath and the Wise Men of Israel.

The wise men of Israel flourished after the voice of prophecy had died in Israel. They studied the world around them as well as the *torah*; but they recognized that true wisdom descends from God as a free gift (Prov 1:23). Ben Sira, a Hebrew wise man who flourished at the beginning of the second century before Christ, believed that only fear, or reverance, for the Lord gives the search for wisdom a firm foundation. That same reverence perfects and crowns its acquisition (Eccles 1:1, 14-20).

The Book of Job likens wisdom to a "Breath of the Almighty" that opens the human heart to an understanding that transcends mere human cleverness (Job 32:8); and the Book of Wisdom makes a similar affirmation (Wis 7:15-22). The latter book also attempts to characterize the wisdom which the Breath of God inspires. Divine wisdom heals anxiety and brings peace to the heart. She inspires kindliness towards others, especially to those needier than oneself. She teaches one to appreciate every authentic value. She opens the mind to all reality, overlooking nothing. She makes one ready to perform good deeds.

In addition, the wisdom born of God's Breath yields a distinctive kind of understanding. She endows those who live wisely with subtlety of mind and heart, sensitizing them to the mystery and complexity of life. Divine wisdom never sanctions anything harmful. On the contrary, true wisdom sanctifies.

Finally, true wisdom manifests its divine origin by the way it operates. True wisdom reflects the divine glory, transforms those who possess it into the beloved of God, and gives them a share in the divine insight which orders all things sweetly. True wisdom inspires every authentic act of piety and every true prophecy (Wis 7:22b-8:1).

Besides portraying the Breath of God as the source and inspiration of every human participation in divine wisdom, the sages of Israel contributed two other important insights into her reality and activity. They associated the divine Breath with God's creative activity, and they identified her with the wisdom of God itself. Moreover, as the wisdom tradition developed, the first of these two insights helped give rise to the second. Let us try to understand how that occurred.

The priestly account of creation which opens the book of Genesis was written during the Babylonian exile, and it assigns to the Breath of God a role within the divine creative act. Unlike the god of the Babylonians who had to struggle against the forces of chaos in order to conquer them, the God of the Hebrews creates by the naked power of his word. He speaks, and creatures spring into existence. Before, however, God utters his first creative word in the first chapter of Genesis, the Breath of God is already active, hovering over the restless waters of chaos, apparently disposing them to hear the words of creation God is about to speak (Gen 1:1-2:3).

The psalms and the writings of the Hebrew wise men extend and embellish this association of the Breath of God with his creative activity. Psalm 104 ascribes to the divine Breath the ongoing creation of life in nature. When God breathes out, life flourishes in the animal kingdom; when he breathes in the animals perish. In other words, in and through His life-giving Breath God becomes present to every living creature (Ps 104:27-30).

Psalm 139 goes even further. It portrays the Breath of God as much more than the source of human religious enlightenment. The psalmist declares that no one can escape the Breath and presence of God. In effect he is asserting that, if we view the Breath of God as an aspect of the divine reality itself, then she functions within the Godhead as a principle of scrutinizing omniscience (Ps 139:7).

The Book of Wisdom develops this same insight even further. The author not only identifies the Breath of God with the divine wisdom itself but also portrays that wisdom as all-encompassing and omniscient. The Breath of wisdom within the Godhead judges human conduct, knows our most secret thoughts and words, and fills the whole world (Wis: 7:15-22).

Finally, in the books of Proverbs and of Wisdom, the divine wisdom undergoes personification as a woman. She addresses the reader in her own name and with divine authority. Like the prophets of old she combs the streets proclaiming enlightenment and seeking new disciples (Prov 1:20-33; Wis 6:22-25, 7:22-30).

The association of the Breath of God with his creative activity in the book of Genesis led, then, to some important developments in the Hebrew understanding of her reality. If the Breath is active in creation, then through her activity God becomes present to his creatures. Since God knows and orders all things by his creative wisdom, as a facet of the divine reality the Breath of divine wisdom should be perceived as the source of divine creative omniscience. The personification of that same wisdom as feminine provides us, as we shall see in the final chapter, with the only personal image of the divine Breath in the entire Bible.

We have reflected on the way in which the Old Testament links breath and life, and we have reflected on the holy Breath of God as a principle of saving enlightenment. We have also pondered what the Hebrew prophets and wise men had to say about her activity and saving reality. Two more tasks confront us. We need to examine how the action of God's Breath in the great leaders of Israel gave rise to the hope for a messiah; and we need to reflect on the challenge which the Old Testament witness to the divine Breath poses in our own day and age.

IV. The Inspired Leader.

The prophets of Israel expressed the inspiration of the Breath of God in words. Israel's charismatic leaders did so in deeds. Moreover, we find evidence that the prophets themselves recognized that the same Breath that inspired them inspired the truly great leaders of Israel. Third Isaiah, for example, proclaimed that God had orchestrated the entire exodus through the sanctifying Breath he had imparted to Moses (Is 63:7-14).

The historical books of the Old Testament also depict Moses as charismatically inspired by the divine Breath. In the book of Numbers Moses, exhausted by the burdens of leading God's people through the desert, asks God for relief. God instructs Him to summon seventy elders to stand around the tent in which the ark of the covenant resides. God then transfers some of the divine Breath present in Moses to the seventy, including two tardy ones who fail to arrive on time at the tent. As a proof of the fact that they now share in the same Breath that inspired Moses, all seventy began to prophesy ecstatically (Num 11:10-30).

The book of Deuteronomy also speaks of a transfer of God's Breath from Moses to Joshua (Deut 34:9). In this latter case the transfer does not empower Joshua to share with Moses the burdens of leading God's people but designates him as the one who will replace Moses after his death.[1]

[1]The book of Deuteronomy also speaks of the transfer of the Breath of prophecy. Elisha, the principal disciple of the prophet Elijah, receives a "double portion" of

Between the conquest of Canaan between 1220 and 1200 B.C. and the establishment of the monarchy in 1030 B.C. the divine Breath inspired judges to lead Israel in moments of crisis. Othoniel, Jephthah, Gideon, and Samson responded to the Breath's enlightenment and led God's people to victory over their enemies (Judg 3:10, 11:29, 6:34, 7:2, 13:25, 14:16, 15:15).

When Saul was anointed the first king of Israel by the prophet Samuel, God confirmed the prophet's choice of Saul by sending to him the Breath of prophecy (1 Sam 9:26-10:13). The divine Breath also played an important role in the story of David's accession to the throne. She remained with king Saul until he disobeyed God. When Samuel then anointed David to replace Saul on the throne of Israel, the divine Breath departed from Saul and rested instead upon David, never to leave him despite his sins and peccadillos (1 Sam 11:5, 16:23).

Messianic Longing.

Solomon, David's successor, like his father took on legendary stature in the shared memories of God's people. Nevertheless, the manifest wickedness of most of the kings of Israel and of Judah disqualified them as plausible bearers of a holy Breath.

Both hope and disillusionment struggled within the prophet Isaiah as he contemplated the careers of David's successors. He prophesied under king Ahaz, one of the wickedest of all the men to sit on the throne of David. In the book of Immanuel, a section of the first part of the book of Isaiah, the prophet responded to Ahaz's iniquity by predicting the birth of another king to succeed him. Isaiah named the successor Immanuel, God-with-us, so abundantly would

the latter's prophetic breath. Under the Deuteronomic code, a firstborn son had the right to a double portion of his father's property (Deut 21:17).

God act through the new king to bless his people (Is 7:10-25).

Isaiah did not live to see the prophecy of Immanuel fulfilled during his own lifetime. At the birth of Hezekiah, Ahaz's son and successor, Isaiah celebrated the event as the birth of one who deserved to be called Wonderful Counselor, Mighty God, Everlasting Father, Prince of Peace (Is 9:1-7). Hezekiah failed to match his father in wickedness; but Isaiah found in him enough malice and venality to know that Immanuel had not yet arrived and that the birth of the Wonderful Counselor and Prince of Peace also lay somewhere in the future. He therefore prophesied yet again, this time predicting the coming of a descendant of David who would possess a plentitude of the divine Breath, a Breath of wisdom and understanding, a Breath of counsel and of might, a Breath of knowledge and fear of the Lord (Is 11:1-2). The Breath-filled king would in effect confront the people as a compendium of all of its great charismatic leaders of old.

Unfulfilled prophecies such as these helped nourish messianic hope in Israel. The prophet Nathan had promised David that God would establish his throne forever (2 Sam 7:1-17). Nevertheless, in 587 B.C. the Babylonians had sacked Jerusalem and deported the last reigning descendant of David into exile.

After the return from exile, devout Jews read and reread the ancient prophecies, wondering when God would finally send the promised descendant of David who would reestablish his throne forever. They called the promised leader the messiah, the anointed one, and looked to find him in promising national leaders. They looked in vain but certain in faith that God would fulfill his word one day.[2]

[2]Jewish messianic longing looked for an "end time," for a period at the end of history when God would fulfill his promises to his people in an era of unparallelled peace and prosperity. The New Testament teaches that the resurrection of Jesus begins the "end time." The Greek word "eschaton" translates the idea of an "end time" and gives rise to the theological term "eschatology." Christian eschatology reflects on the "end" or fulfillment of the salvation begun in the death and resurrection of Jesus. Initially, Christian eschatology expressed the ultimate hope of Christians for the second coming of Christ; but, as the expectation faded that Jesus

Other passages in the Old Testament fed messianic hopes. Third Isaiah had described his own prophetic commissioning as something like a royal anointing by the divine Breath that empowered him:

> to bring good tidings to the afflicted; he has sent me to bind up the brokenhearted, to proclaim liberty to captives, and the opening of the prison to those who are bound; to proclaim the year of the Lord's favor and the day of vengeance of our God, to comfort all who mourn. . . . (Is 61:1-2).

When the Anointed came he would surely accomplish all these things. But when?

The first Christians would find all of these prophecies fulfilled in Jesus. They would, moreover, draw on another Old Testament text in order to understand his ministry, death, and resurrection. They would identify him with the obscure figure of the servant of God whom second Isaiah described in a series of moving songs. A prophetic figure anointed by the Breath of God, the servant atones for the sins of God's people by his innocent suffering and death. God, however, vindicates his servant by restoring him to life and by acting through him to establish his just reign on earth (Is 42:1-9, 49:1-6, 50:4-9, 52:12-53:12).

The Challenge of The Old Testament Witness to God's Breath.

Believing that something exists or holds true differs in significant ways from believing in someone or something. We may believe that something exists without its existence making any personal difference to us. I may believe, for example, that boabab trees grow in Africa without that belief

would return soon, Christian eschatological thinking tended to focus on "the four last things": viz., death, judgment, heaven, and hell.

changing my life significantly. The boabab's flourishing makes no practical difference to the way I choose to live. Its germination makes no personal claims upon me. It exacts of me no personal commitment.

The persons and realities we believe in, however, do make claims upon us. They command our loyalty and commitment. The way we relate to them changes the way we live our lives. When I believe in a person, for example, I endorse what that person stands for. I commit myself to taking that person very seriously. I trust the individual in question. I expect someone I believe in to live up to certain expectations. I also depend personally on those in whom I choose to believe.

When, for example, we Americans publicly honor a national religious leader like Martin Luther King, we endorse the vision for which he stood, we take very seriously his insight into the problems facing a nation like ours and into the way we ought to go about solving those problems. We expect such national leaders to live up to the ideals and vision they endorse, and we acknowledge that we depend on their insight and guidance.

Christians believe that the Holy Breath of God exists. In addition, however, they also claim to believe in her. Believing in the Breath of God makes very practical claims upon the way we go about living our lives both as individuals and as members of the Christian community. It demands of us that we respond to her every enlightenment. It requires that we relate to her with the absolute and ultimate trust and expectant faith that a divine person deserves. Believing in the Breath of God commits us to living in life-long responsiveness to her divine guidance and empowerment.

The Old Testament yields some important insights into the practical implications of believing in the divine Breath. Those who believe in God's Holy Breath look to her as a divine source of life and enlightenment. They cultivate through personal prayer and through active participation in worshiping communities sensitivity to the full spectrum of her divine inspirations. They look to her to sustain their faith in God, to teach them how to pray, to live in fidelity to the covenant they have sealed with God.

Moreover, the Breath of God who raised up prophets to Israel continues to pour out prophetic inspiration on contemporary believers. The charismatic renewal began in the late 1960's as a movement within Catholic lay spirituality; but it has since spread to all the main-line Christian churches. The movement now numbers members in virtually every continent. In addition, the charismatic renewal has effected something like a renewal of ecstatic prophecy in contemporary Christian churches. The kind of prophecy cultivated in charismatic prayer groups does not, to be sure, reproduce all the details of ecstatic prophecy in the Old Testament; but it does resemble the ecstatic prophecy there described enough to warrant a comparison.

Moreover, the Breath of Christ is also raising up other prophetic voices within the contemporary churches, voices that remind us of the writing prophets of the OT. The writing prophets, as we have seen, confronted in God's name the major social, political, and economic issues of their day. They summoned their contemporaries to acknowledge the injustice and sinfulness of their ways and to return to faithful obedience to the covenant they had made with God. In our own day individuals like Martin Luther King, Dorothy Day, and Daniel Berrigan have exercised a similar prophetic ministry; and like the Old Testament writing prophets they have suffered for challenging institutional injustice and oppression while armed only with the word of God.

Liberation theologians in this country and in the developing nations are speaking a similar prophetic word about the need to reform the structures of economic, racial, sexual, and political oppression that enslave and degrade millions of human beings. In their most recent pastoral letters the North American bishops have also spoken a prophetic word by denouncing racism, by calling for nuclear disarmament and an end to the arms race, by demanding the reform of the United States economy in a way that ensures justice for all people.

Were the writing prophets of the Old Testament alive today, they would most certainly summon people who claim to believe in God to deal with the same kinds of economic, social, and political issues which contemporary prophetic voices are addressing; for they did no less in their own day. That suggestion should come as no surprise, for the Breath of God who breathed in them continues to breathe prophetically in the hearts of contemporary believers. Those, then, who claim to believe in God's Holy Breath belie themselves if they fail to hearken to the voice of prophecy as it sounds in the churches today.

In our own day, the Breath of prophecy also inspires words of consolation and of hope, just as she did during the Babylonian exile. Since the invention of atomic weapons these engines of destruction have held the people of this planet hostage to the arms race and to the threat of global annihilation. At the second Vatican council and in *The Challenge of Peace*, the North American bishops' pastoral on nuclear disarmament, the Breath of God has spoken through church leaders in order to remind us that we have, if we are willing to take them, the means within our power to choose life rather than self-annihilation in a nuclear holocaust. We can choose to make peace with justice rather than to continue a proliferation of nuclear weapons that increasingly call into question human survival rather than guarantee it.

In the chapters which follow we shall have occasion to examine in greater detail the message which these and other prophetic voices are speaking to contemporary believers. Here it suffices to note that if we take the Old Testament witness to the divine Breath seriously we cannot in conscience ignore the prophets she raises up in our own day.

Besides calling us to respond to the prophetic voices and charismatic leadership which God's Breath is inspiring in the church today, the Old Testament witness to her saving activity poses another important contemporry religious challenge. The Old Testament uniformly attributes every form of religious enlightenment to the breath of God. As we shall soon see, so does the New Testament. Unless contemporary Christians are willing to do the same, they cannot truly claim to believe in the third person of the trinity; for belief in God's Holy Breath takes on practical meaning when we look to her as the source of all religious enlightenment.

Nevertheless, for a variety of historical reasons which need not detain us for the moment, since the second century western Christians have on the whole preferred to attribute religious enlightenment to the second person of the trinity rather than to the third. In the chapters which follow, I shall attempt to show that this tendency marks a serious aberration in Christian piety. As we shall see in the next chapter, the son of God confronts us historically as the one through whom the triune God speaks and acts in redeeming and saving us. A sound biblical piety, however, perceives the Holy Breath as our present source of religious enlightenment.

Like the Hebrew sages we must, then, look to her to teach us the wisdom of God. Like the wise men of old we need to study and understand the world around us; but if we hope to probe the ultimate significance of human life and of all created reality, we must seek that kind of wisdom from God. We must look to the divine Breath to heal the anxiety and other disordered affections that blind our minds and hearts. We must beseech her to teach us kindness and compassion especially to those in greatest need, to appreciate every authentic value, to grow in readiness to undertake any good work. We must look to Her to sensitize us to the mystery and complexity of life, to instruct us in holiness, to lead us from an understanding of God's creation to a vision of divine glory.

Finally, as we have already seen, the Breath's action in the great leaders of Israel eventually inspired Jewish messianic hope. We cannot, however, understand adequately the practical implications of this important strain in the Old Testament witness to her saving action until we ponder the fulfillment of Jewish messianic expectations in Jesus Christ. To this important question we turn in the chapter which follows.

2

God Breathes on Jesus

In the last chapter we reflected on what the Bible tells us about the action of God's Breath in the Old Testament. In the present chapter we will ponder what the four gospels tell us about her action in Jesus. The chapter divides into five parts. The first four sections summarize what each of the gospels tells us about Jesus' relationship to the Holy Breath. The fifth and final section ponders the points of agreement, convergence, and complementarity in the gospel witness to the Holy Breath.

I. Mark's Witness to the Breath.

Mark's gospel opens with a brief account of the ministry of John the Baptist which culminates in the Baptist's prophecy that another would come after him, "mightier" than himself, who would baptize people not just with water, as John himself had done, but with a sanctifying Breath (Mk 1:7-8).

The account of Jesus' baptism follows immediately. Moreover, Mark narrates the event in such a way as to make it plain that Jesus will fulfill John's prophecy. Immediately after his baptism by John, Jesus experiences a vision. He sees the heavens rent, and the Breath descending on him in the form of a dove. At the same time he hears a voice from heaven proclaim to him: "You are my beloved Son; with you I am well pleased" (Mk 1:9-11). In other words the Holy Breath of God descends on Jesus in order to begin his revelation as the "mightier one" whom John had foretold.

The images which Mark uses in describing Jesus' baptism have symbolic meaning. The rending of the heavens recalls two prophecies of third Isaiah in which this cosmic event presages the beginning of God's final and decisive act of grace and salvation (Is 63:7, 74:11). The Breath of God, therefore, descends on Jesus to transform him into God's instrument for accomplishing decisively the salvation third Isaiah had promised.

The Breath descends under the sign of a dove. The Hebrews kept doves as pets; and rabbinic literature refers to Israel as the dove of God, as his pet and the object of his special delight. Accordingly, the voice from heaven assures Jesus that he is the beloved of God, in whom the Father finds great pleasure. In other words, the Holy Breath descends to begin Jesus' revelation as the beloved of God and as the beginning of a new Israel (Cf. Ps 74:19).

The Breath of God hovering over the baptismal waters recalls, however, the first chapter of Genesis when she breathed over the waters of chaos to dispose them to hear God's creative word. The Holy Breath, therefore, also comes to Jesus to transform him into the beginning of a new creation.

The dove over the waters also reminds one of the story of the flood in Genesis. In that story a dove bearing an olive branch in its mouth returned to Noah and his family in the ark. The return of the dove revealed to them that the flood waters were receding. Moreover, the receding waters foreshadowed the covenant which God would make with Noah and his descendants forever (Gen 8:6-22). The dove hovering over Jesus' baptismal waters suggests, then, that through the action of the Holy Breath in Jesus God will seal a new and everlasting covenant with humankind, but one which transcends utterly his covenant with Noah.

Finally, the descent of the divine Breath on Jesus probably recalls two prophecies from the book of Isaiah. It recalls Isaiah's messianic prophecy that a king, so filled with God's Breath as to be a compendium of all the great charismatic leaders of Israel, would one day come and lead God's people to peace and prosperity (Is 11:9-11). The Breath's descent also recalls the prophecy of third Isaiah that an anointed leader would come to proclaim a season of liberation and jubilee (Is 61:1-4).

Mark's account of Jesus' baptism contains two other biblical references. The voice from heaven combines two texts from the Old Testament. In psalm 2, a messianic psalm, we find the phrase: "You are my son, today I have begotten you" (Ps 2:7), while the first of the servant songs written by second Isaiah begins with these words: "Behold my servant whom I uphold, my chosen in whom my soul delights" (Is 42:1). The voice from heaven combines the first part of the verse from psalm 2 and the second part of the verse from the first servant song. The double citation indicates that the divine Breath has come to transform Jesus into the promised messiah but that in the discharge of his messianic ministry he will also stand revealed as the servant of God who atones for sins by his innocent suffering. It comes, then, as no surprise that in Mark's gospel Jesus refers to his passion and death as the completion of his baptismal anointing (Mk 10:38).

Jesus Tempted In Mark.

Moreover, in Mark's gospel the events which immediately follow upon Jesus' baptism underscore the fact that the divine Breath who empowers his messianic career will also strengthen him to confront the powers of evil that will conspire to thwart and kill him. The baptismal Breath immediately drives Jesus into the wilderness. "And he was in the wilderness forty days tempted by Satan; and he was with the wild beasts; and the angels ministered to him" (Mk 1:12-13).

Once again Mark describes Jesus' temptation in the wilderness with images freighted with theological significance.

The wilderness into which Jesus is driven recalls the second chapter of Genesis, when God transformed a wilderness into a beautiful garden, created Adam as its gardener, and led the beasts to him for naming (Gen 2:4-25). Jesus, designated in his baptism as the beginning of a new creation stands in the wilderness like a new Adam surrounded by the beasts.

Like the first Adam, however, Jesus must also confront Satan, the ancient tempter. The beasts surrounding Jesus also have sinister connotations. The Jews feared wilderness places as the haunt of death-dealing demonic forces, which they symbolized by the strange and powerful desert animals who lived there (Lev 16:10, Is 13:21, 14:23, 30:6, 34:11-16; Zeph 2:13ff). The ministering angels sent to Jesus come apparently to support him in his initial struggle with these powers of evil.

Jesus' struggle foreshadows not only his own death but also the temptations and persecutions which his disciples will face. Mark, who seems to have written his gospel for Christians persecuted under Nero, probably intended the beasts that surround Jesus to remind his readers of the beasts of the Roman arena which devoured the Christian martyrs.

We find only three other references to the Holy Breath in Mark's gospel. One need not detain us long. At one point Jesus alludes to the fact that the Breath of God inspired David to write the psalms (Mk 12:36). The text makes it clear that Mark regards the divine Breath that inspired Jesus' ministry as identical with the Holy Breath God had breathed on Israel.

Significantly, however, the other two references to the Breath of God in Mark's gospel allude to the struggle against demons and the forces of anti-Christ. Both texts underscore the fact that those moved by the Breath of Christ must expect personal confrontation with the forces of evil.

Jesus and Beelzebul in Mark.

In the first text, Jesus' enemies charge that his power to

cast out demons proves that he himself is possessed by Beelzebul, the prince of devils. Jesus refutes the slander with a two-pronged argument. First he notes that if Satan is indeed working against himself by casting out his own devils, his kingdom is crumbling. Having unmasked his adversaries' inconsistency, Jesus then turns the argument against them. In fact, he points out, his power over demons reveals that he is mightier than Satan and his minions, that he is, in effect, the "mightier one" whom John the Baptist had foretold. He then warns his adversaries that in attributing the work of the divine Breath within him to Beelzebul, they blaspheme her. He also warns that those who close their hearts to her action blind themselves to God's saving action in this life and court damnation in the next (Mk 3:28-29).

The Breath of Witness.

In the second text referring to the divine Breath, Jesus warns his disciples that like him they must face suffering and persecution, but he assures them that they need not fear persecution since the same divine Breath that inspired him will empower them to testify boldly in his name (Mk 13:9-11).

Clearly, even though we do not find extensive references to God's Breath in Mark's gospel, the references the evangelist does make enunciate some important claims about Jesus. Jesus after his baptism receives his messianic commission from the Father in the power of the Holy Breath whom he will one day communicate to his own disciples. She comes to reveal him as the beloved of God and beginning of a new Israel, as the new Adam who begins a new creation. She also comes to strengthen him to confront and overcome Satan and the forces of evil. Jesus' conflict with the powers of darkness will culminate in his own passion and death. The divine Breath comes therefore to reveal him as messiah in the image of the suffering servant described by second Isaiah. Moreover, for Mark those who possess the same Breath as inspired Jesus' in his ministry can expect to be drawn into conflict with the same forces that put him to death; but they can also expect the Breath of Christ to strengthen them to overcome Satan and his minions as Jesus did.

Behind Mark's understanding of the action of God's Breath in both Jesus and in his disciples stands the grim reality of the cross. The Breath of Jesus comes to his disciples in order to draw them into his passion. The starkness of Mark's vision reflects the experience of a community which risked martyrdom on a day-to-day basis. When read in that context, Mark's portrayal of the Holy Breath's action in both Jesus and his followers would have been read as he intended: namely, as a message of encouragement and of hope. No matter what they might suffer for confessing Christ, the members of Mark's community would have known that the Breath which inspired their witness to Jesus made them into members of the Israel of God and communicated to them the risen life of the new Adam.

II. The Baptismal Breath in Matthew.

Matthew the evagelist based his gospel on some version of the gospel of Mark. Mark's gospel begins with the story of Jesus' baptism and messianic anointing by the Holy Breath. Because Mark says nothing about Jesus' relationship to the divine Breath prior to his baptism, Mark's readers might have inferred that his relationship to her began at the moment John baptized him. Matthew's gospel takes pains to set aside any such misconception. The infancy narrative which opens Matthew's gospel asserts clearly that Jesus was miraculously conceived of a virgin by the power of the divine Breath (Mt 1:20).

In insisting that Jesus stood in relationship to the Breath of God from the first moment of his conception, Matthew rejects the error of adoptionism which asserts that Jesus was just an ordinary human being prior to his baptism and only became God's adopted son when the Holy Breath descended on him at the Jordan. Far from portraying Jesus as God's adopted son, Matthew holds him up as Immanuel, as God-with-us. Moreover, in Matthew's gospel Jesus will finally fulfill the prophecy of Immanuel when as the risen Christ he sends his disciples to baptize all creatures in the name of Father, Son, and Breath, while simultaneously promising that he will be with them to the end of the world (28:18-20).

Matthew, however, endorsed the main lines of Mark's account of Jesus baptism as well as Mark's theological understanding of the saving significance of that event. Nevertheless, Matthew modified Mark's text in significant ways that yield an insight into his distinctive interpretation of Jesus' relationship to the Breath of God.

For example, Matthew, citing in all likelihood a more primitive version of the Baptist's prophecy, has John promise that the mightier one who will follow John will baptize with a Holy Breath "and with fire" (Mt 3:11). In Matthew as in Mark the Breath of God will come to Jesus in his baptism under the sign of a dove in order to reveal him as the beloved son of God and beginning of a new Israel. She will, however, come to Jesus' disciples not under the sign of a dove but under the sign of fire.

Fire symbolizes the holiness of God which purifies the sinfulness of those who believe in him and which stands in judgment over those who reject him. Clearly, in Matthew's eyes the Holy Breath relates in one way to Jesus and in another to his disciples.

Matthew also modifies Mark's account of Jesus' baptism. He does not describe it, although he admits that it occurred (Mt 3:13, 16). Moreover, before John baptizes Jesus, the two discuss the propriety of what John is about to do. The fact that Jesus had been baptized by another religious leader seems to have embarrassed the first Christians; and in the dialogue between Jesus and John Matthew offers a theological interpretation of that event which makes clear the superiority of Christian baptism to the baptism which John administered.

Matthew's John tries to prevent Jesus from accepting his baptism with the words: "I need to be baptized by you, and do you come to me?" Jesus, however, brushes aside the objection, saying: "Let it be so now; for thus it is fitting to fulfill all righteousness" (Mt 3:14-15).

Jesus' words link his baptism to a major theme in Matthew's gospel: namely, the theme of fulfillment. In Matthew's eyes Jesus comes to fulfill the law and the prophets (Mt 5:17). He does so by requiring of his followers all that the law demands and more.

Matthew's infancy narrative alludes frequently to Jesus' fulfillment of the Hebrew scriptures (Mt 1:22-23, 2:5-6, 17-18). Jesus also comes to fulfill John's own prophetic ministry. This he will accomplish when he fulfills John' prophecy about the coming of a mightier Breath-baptizer. Moreover, Matthew's Jesus will fulfill John's prediction by rising from the dead and sending his own disciples to baptize all people in the triune name (Mt 28:18-20). Jesus' baptism at the hands of another religious leader can, then, be tolerated for "now" because Christian baptism will one day "fulfill all righteousness" by fulfilling the meaning of John's own baptism.

In Mark's account of Jesus' baptism the voice from heaven speaks directly to Jesus. Matthew, however, has it speak to the reader and through the reader to the world. In thus modifying Mark's text Matthew summons his readers to confess their faith in Jesus as the Son of God and messiah in the image of the suffering servant of second Isaiah (Mt 3:17). In every other respect, however, Matthew endorses Mark's account of Jesus' baptism.

Jesus Tempted in Matthew.

On the other hand, Matthew drastically changes Mark's account of Jesus' temptations. As in Mark's temptation narrative, the Breath of God leads Jesus into the desert to be tempted. The reference to the action of the divine Breath in Jesus at the beginning of his temptation links that event to his baptism and to the theme of fulfillment which Matthew has stressed in his account of that event. In other respects, however, Matthew alters Mark's account of Jesus' temptation. We find in Matthew no reference to desert animals as we do in Mark. Instead Matthew transforms Mark's cryptic reference to Satan into an extended and dramatic dialogue between Jesus and the tempter. The key to understanding Matthew's temptation narrative lies in understanding the meaning of that dialogue.

In Matthew as in Mark Jesus confronts Satan not simply as an individual but as the beginning of a new Israel. As the embodiment of all that the new Israel is called by God to become, Jesus in his temptations stands before his disciples as their model. The temptations he knows they will know as well. In the power of the Breath that dwelt in him and which he will send them they must respond to temptation as he responded.

Here we should note that for Matthew as for Mark the Holy Breath which the Messiah will send his followers will seek to conform them to his image. In both Matthew and Mark she does this by drawing them into his passion. Matthew, however, more than Mark insists that openness to the Holy Breath involves more than receptivity to her charisms. It demands more fundamentally obedience to Jesus' moral vision (Mt 7:21-23); for Matthew's Jesus fulfills the law by proclaiming a new covenant which demands more of his followers than the old covenant did of the Jews. Indeed, Matthew, with scribal care will in the course of his gospel group the teachings of Jesus into five major discourses.

The story of Jesus' baptism and temptations functions, then, in Matthew's as in Mark's gospel as a preface to Jesus' entire public ministry. Everything Jesus says and does in his public ministry should, therefore, be interpreted in the light of the story of his baptismal commissioning and subsequent temptation. In this context, it is important that in his temptations not only does Matthew's Jesus act in the power of the divine Breath whom he will send his followers in order to teach them covenant fidelity, but Jesus also triumphs over Satan precisely by designating those very precepts of the law which his own teaching and example will fulfill.

What, then, do Jesus' temptations signify, and how does his moral teaching fulfill their significance in Matthew's account of his ministry?

Jesus' Moral Message.

In Matthew's temptation narrative Satan first tempts Jesus to use his messianic power to end his fast, change stones into bread, and eat (Mt 4:1-3). Mark makes no mention of Jesus' fast; Matthew does. What does the fast mean, and why does Satan want Jesus to end it?

Devout Jews fasted, not in order to gain control over their appetite for food, but as a way of recalling the desert wanderings of their people, when they depended from day to day upon God to sustain them in life (Ex 16: 1ff). Jesus has undertaken a fast in the wilderness as a way of entering into the experience of the first Israel and of expressing his trust in the Father to sustain and protect him in the fulfillment of his messianic mission. When, therefore, Satan urges Jesus to use his miraculous powers to end the fast, he is tempting Jesus to abandon dependence on the Father and replace it with personal self-reliance. Satan is equivalently saying, "If you intend to obey the voice that spoke to you in your baptism, then, don't trust in it, trust in yourself instead."

Jesus' reply to Satan makes it clear that we should interpret the first temptation in this sense. He answers, "Man shall not live by bread alone, but by every word that proceeds from the mouth of God" (Mt 4:5). As the beginning of a new Israel Jesus thus warns his followers against sinful self-reliance and exemplifies for them instead trust in the Father's providential care.

Moreover, in the course of Matthew's gospel, Jesus will demand just such a trust of his disciples. "Look at the birds of the air: they neither sow nor reap nor gather into barns and yet your heavenly Father feeds them. Are you not of more value than they?" (Mt 6:25-34). His disciples must seek their bread in trust from God each day (Mt 6:11).

In addition, Matthew's Jesus demands that his followers let trust in God's care free them from finding false security in riches. Instead, they must share their possessions freely with those in greater need. Such sharing embodies concretely faith in the reign of God which Jesus' ministry begins and proclaims (Mt 25:31-36).

Having failed to seduce Jesus into self-reliance rather than trust in the Father, Satan next tempts him to test God (Mt 4:4-6). To test God means to set the conditions under which one is willing to trust him. Once again Jesus rejects the temptation outright: "You shall not tempt the Lord your God" (Mt 4:7).

In other words, Jesus as the beginning of the new Israel embodies not just trust in God but unconditioned trust. Moreover, Matthew's Jesus will require a similar trust of his disciples (Mt 10:26-33).

If, however, in Jesus' vision of the kingdom faith in God finds concrete expression in the willingness to share one's physical possessions with others, then unconditioned faith would logically require an unconditioned willingness to share. Does Matthew's Jesus require such sharing of his disciples?

He does in the sense that one must place no condition in principle on one's willingness to share. One must share not just on the basis of merit but also and especially on the basis of need. One must share even with one's enemies (Mt 5:38-42). Moreover, willingness to share one's possessions with sinners, the marginal, and the outcast imitates the perfection of the Father's love who sends the blessings of this life to saint and sinner alike (Mt 5:43-48).

In Jesus' third and final temptation in the desert, Satan urges him to found the kingdom of God on coercive power and promises to give Jesus all the kingdoms of the world if he will only fall down in worship before his tempter (Mt 4:8-9). Jesus rejects the idolatrous offer outright, insisting that the reign of God can be founded only on authentic worship of the Father (Mt 4:10-11).

Moreover, Matthew's Jesus makes similar moral demands

of his disciples. They must renounce the exercise of worldly power by refusing to lord it over one another in the manner of gentile kings. Instead, they must serve one another in the image of Jesus who lays down his life for his disciples (Mt 18:21-22). Instead of founding the kingdom on coercive power, Matthew's Jesus founds it on worship of the Father (Mt 6:7-13); but authentic worship requires as its condition a willingness to forgive one another in atoning love: "So, if you are offering your gift at the altar and there remember that your brother has something against you, leave your gift there before the altar and go; first be reconciled to your brother and then come and offer your gift" (Mt 5:23-24, 6:12).

Clearly, Matthew's elaboration of Mark's temptation narrative has important practical consequences for Christian living. A careful reading of Mark's gospel will show that his Jesus proclaims the same set of religious values as Matthew's. Matthew, however, links the proclamation of new covenant morality more explicitly than Mark to the presence within Jesus of the divine Breath. Matthew's Jesus in his desert temptations conquers Satan in the power of the Breath that descended on him in his baptism and which he will send his disciples. Moreover, under her inspiration he vanquishes the tempter by citing those precepts of the law that his own moral teaching will especially fulfill. For Matthew, then, when Jesus baptizes his disciples with the Holy Breath, she will come to empower them to conquer the evil one not only by witnessing to Jesus under persecution but also by faithful obedience to the ethics of discipleship which Jesus exemplified and proclaimed.

Markan Parallels.

Matthew like Mark recounts the incident in which Jesus' enemies accuse him of casting out demons by the power of Beelzebul. Matthew does not deviate significantly from Mark's version of that encounter (Mt 12:22-32). Matthew, however, underscores the blindness of Jesus' slanderers by prefacing the story of their accusation with an account of multiple miracles performed by Jesus, miracles which reveal him as the servant of God anointed by the divine Breath to speak judgment to the nations (Mt 12:15-21; Is 42:1-4). In refuting the charge of possession, Jesus passes judgment on the unbelief of his enemies. Moreover, by portraying Jesus' exorcisms as a sign of the arrival of God's reign, Matthew implicitly links them to Jesus' victory over Satan in his third temptation in the desert (Mt 12:28).

Finally, Matthew's Jesus like Mark's promises his disciples that in times of persecution the Breath of the Father will teach them how to bear witness to him (Mt 10:20). Matthew, however, insists more explicitly than Mark that Jesus himself abides with his church in a way that is permanent, direct, and immediate (Mt 28:18-20).

III. God's Breath in Luke's Gospel.

Luke, like Matthew opposes an adoptionist reading of Jesus' baptism and asserts that Jesus stood in a graced relationship to the Breath of God from the first moment of his conception. Moreover, in Luke's account of the annunciation the angel promises Mary that the Breath of God "will come upon you and the power of the Most High will overshadow you; therefore the child to be born will be called holy, the Son of God" (Lk 1:35). The images which the angel uses suggest that the Breath's descent will transform Mary into a living temple, the very dwelling place of God.

The tone of the angel's words also implies that in conceiving Jesus, the Breath of God will inaugurate the last age of salvation. Here too, Luke qualifies Mark's gospel, which associates the inauguration of the last age of salvation with Jesus' baptism. Luke not only begins the eschatological era with Jesus conception, but he will attenuate the eschatological tone of his narrative of Jesus' baptism by having the Breath of God descend on him in bodily form (Lk 3:22).

Moreover, Luke describes a great outpouring of God's Breath which accompanies the birth of the messiah. She inspires Elizabeth to proclaim Mary blessed among women and mother of the Lord (Lk 1:42), Zechariah to prophesy that John the Baptist will conduct his ministry in the image of Elijah (Lk 1:67), and Simeon to predict that Jesus will know conflict and contradiction and effect "the fall and rising of many in Israel" (Lk 2:34).

The references to God's Breath in Luke's infancy narrative occur in passages that foreshadow a number of themes that Luke will develop in his account of Jesus' baptism: the exclusion of adoptionism, the inauguration of the last age of salvation, the revelation of Jesus as messiah, the primacy of Jesus' mission over John's, the fact that Jesus would suffer as messiah. The abundance of the Breath's inspirations in the infancy narrative also anticipate her final eschatological outpouring on Pentecost day (Acts 1:16, 2:30).

The Baptismal Breath in Luke.

Luke like Matthew contrasts Jesus' relationship to the Breath of God with the way she relates to his disciples. As in Matthew's gospel she comes to Jesus under the sign of a dove to reveal him as the beloved of God and beginning of a new Israel; but she comes to his disciples under the sign of fire: in purification and judgment (Lk 2:16-17, 23).

Luke also states that Jesus' messianic vision and commissioning in the power of the divine Breath occurred only after John had finished baptizing and while Jesus was praying (Lk 3:21). In separating the two events, Luke makes it clear that John's baptism in no way caused Jesus' messianic anointing and commissioning. The evangelist may also have desired to draw a parallel between the baptismal Breath's descent on Jesus and her arrival on Pentecost. In Acts she descends on the disciples as they are gathered in the upper room, apparently in prayer (Acts 1:14).

On the whole, however, Luke like Matthew endorses the

main lines of Mark's theological understanding of Jesus' baptism, for like Matthew Luke derives his gospel in part from some version of Mark's account of Jesus' ministry. As we have seen, Luke underplays the eschatological tone of his narrative of Jesus' baptism. Nevertheless, as in Mark Jesus' heavenly commissioning in Luke begins his public revelation as messiah, Son of God, suffering servant, Breath-baptizer, new Adam, and the beginning of a new creation.

Jesus Tempted in Luke.

Luke separates his account of Jesus' baptism from his temptations by a geneology that traces Jesus' origins all the way back to Adam, who is called "son of God." Matthew who wrote for a community of Jewish Christians had traced Jesus' family tree back to Abraham (Mt 1:1-17). Luke's geneology reflects the theme of universal salvation which recurs in his gospel and in Acts: as messianic "Son of God," Jesus, the new Adam, proclaims a salvation so universal in scope that it seeks nothing less than the graced recreation of the entire human race (Lk 3:23-38).

Luke like Matthew describes the encounter between Jesus and Satan in the desert in considerable detail. Luke insists more than Matthew that Satan really does exercise dominion over the kingdoms of this world (Lk 4:1-13); but he departs from Matthew's temptation narrative principally in the way in which he orders the three temptations. In Luke the temptation to test God comes last (Lk 4:9-12).

Luke reorders Jesus' temptations for three theological reasons. First, the temptation to test God takes place on the pinnacle of the temple in Jerusalem. Satan tells Jesus to hurl himself to the ground as a way of forcing God to save him. Jerusalem and the temple play an important role in Luke's gospel narrative. He portrays Jesus' ministry as the movement of the gospel from Galilee to Jerusalem, just as Acts will portray its movement from Jerusalem, the center of the Jewish world, to Rome, the center of the gentile world. The movement of the temptation narrative follows a similar pattern: Jesus' temptations culminate in Jerusalem. Second, by placing Jesus' last temptation in Jerusalem Luke can portray it as a foreshadowing of Jesus' passion. Satan, vanquished, leaves Jesus to return at "an opportune time," namely, at the time of his passion which also occurs in the holy city (Lk 4:13). Third, in placing the temptation to test God last Luke is attempting to signal to his readers that he regards the temptation to test God, to put conditions on one's willingness to trust him, as the supreme temptation of Jesus' followers. Let us ponder this last Lukan insight in greater detail.

Luke's Jesus proclaims the same ethics of discipleship as Matthew's and Mark's. Like the other synoptic evangelists, Luke regards the willingness to share one's personal possessions with the needy as the most immediate practical consequence of faith and trust in the Father's providential care. Such sharing introduces one into the kingdom and will find a special reward in the life to come (Lk 16:9, 12:22-34, 16:10-13, 18:28-30).

Luke's Jesus excoriates the Pharisees' love of wealth as an "abomination," a loathsome thing, in God's eyes (Lk 16:14-15, 12-39). Not only does attachment to wealth enslave one in ways that exclude one from God's kingdom, it renders the service of God impossible (Lk 16:13, 18:18-27). Gross avarice plunges one into the fires of Gehenna (Lk 16:19-31) and contradicts faith in the resurrection (Lk 16:31). On the other hand, willingness to live poorly with a servant messiah expresses true discipleship (Lk 14:33); and hospitality toward the poor will find its special reward in the resurrection of the just (Lk 14:12-14, 21).

In his account of Jesus' desert temptations, Luke like Matthew portrays Jesus as exemplifying for the new Israel he begins an unconditioned faith in God. Moreover, like Matthew Luke insists that an unconditioned trust in God's providential care finds practical expression in the unrestricted scope of Christian faith-sharing. Jesus' disciples must not only give alms; they must also welcome the outcast and dispossessed into their very homes (Lk 10:57-58, 14:12-14).

For Luke as for Matthew the willingness to share one's goods with a gratuity of love that imitates God's own love even of sinners validates the Christian claim to live as a child of God in Jesus' image (Lk 6:32-36).

Finally, like Matthew Luke founds the kingdom of God, not on power politics, but on a worship whose authenticity is measured by personal repentance and mutual forgiveness (Lk 5:32, 6:36-37, 11:3, 17:4).

As we have seen, Matthew promised that the Holy Breath would teach the disciples of Jesus obedience to the ethics of discipleship which he lived and proclaimed. In Acts Luke describes how she does so. The three thousand converts baptized on Pentecost give evidence of their openness to the divine Breath by accepting the moral demands of Christian discipleship:

> And they devoted themselves to the apostles' teaching and fellowship, to the breaking of bread and the prayers. . . .- And all who believed were together and had all things in common; and they sold their possessions and goods and distributed them to all. And attending the temple together and breaking bread in their homes, they partook of food with glad and generous hearts, praising God and having favor with all the people (Acts 2:41-47).

The Jerusalem community's faithful adherence to a gospel morality contrasts sharply with the stinginess of Ananias and Sapphira. The unfortunate couple sells their property and claims to turn over to the apostles all the proceeds of the sale for distribution to the poor. In fact, they secretly keep some of the money for themselves (Acts 5:1-2).

Knowing their deceit, Peter confronts Ananias and accuses him of "testing God." The accusation recalls Jesus' final, culminating temptation in the desert. Like Jesus Ananias and his wife are being sifted by Satan; but unlike Jesus they succumb to his third and greatest temptation (Acts 5:3).

How did Ananias and Sapphira test God? As we have seen, for Luke as for Matthew one tests God by setting conditions on one's willingness to trust him; and unconditioned trust in God requires the freedom of heart to share one's goods gratuitously with others not on the basis of merit only but also and especially on the basis of need. In their lying failure to share all of their possessions with the needy members of the Jerusalem community, Ananias and Sapphira stand convicted of setting conditions on their willingness to trust God. Moreover, Luke contrasts their cupidity with the generosity of Barnabas, the "son of encouragement" (Acts 4:32-5:11).

The story of Ananias and Sapphira also illustrates what it means to say that the Breath of God comes to the disciples of Jesus under the sign of fire. Fire symbolizes the holiness of God in its capacity to purify or judge human sinfulness. Peter pronounces judgment over the unlucky couple for having sinfully tested God. At the word of judgment both of them drop dead, punished for having lied to the Breath of God (Acts 5:3-4, 9).

Clearly, then, Luke regarded the temptation to "test God" as the supreme temptation of the followers of Jesus. Jesus himself faced that temptation last of all in the desert and confronted it again on Calvary. In their daily lives, however, Christians test God when they falsify the authentic inspirations of the Breath of Christ by clinging to worldly possessions as the ultimate source of their security instead of sharing their goods freely with those in greatest need.

Luke the evangelist wrote for a community that was beginning to doubt that the second coming of Christ would happen soon. The church he knew had begun to settle more comfortably into this world: too comfortably, Luke thought. He therefore excoriated any sign of worldliness in those who claimed to follow Jesus. One can only wonder how he would have reacted to the worldly affluence of some contemporary Christians.

The Breath of God in Jesus.

Luke insists more explicitly than either Matthew or Mark

that Jesus conducted his entire public ministry under the inspiration and guidance of the divine Breath (Lk 4:14-15). Luke underscores this point when he concludes his account of Jesus' early ministry with the story of his preaching at Nazareth. Invited to speak in the synagogue of his home town, Jesus unrolls the scroll of the Hebrew scripture to a prophecy of third Isaiah which promises that the messiah will in the power of God's Breath preach good news to the poor, release to captives, the recovery of sight to the blind, liberty to the oppressed, and a universal season of jubilee. Jesus then claims that his own ministry fulfills that prophecy (Lk 4:16-19; Is 61:1-2).

Moreover, in the course of narrating the rest of Jesus' ministry, Luke makes it clear that God's Breath inspires both his unique messianic awareness as Son of God and the divine wisdom he embodies and proclaims (Lk 10:21-22). Luke's Jesus also assures his disciples that the Father will give the Holy Breath to anyone who seeks her in prayer (Lk 11:13). Jesus' promise will be abundantly fulfilled when the divine Breath descends on the disciples assembled on Pentecost day (Acts 2:1-4).

Jesus and Beelzebul in Luke.

Despite his insistence on the Breath's action in Jesus, nevertheless, in narrating the confrontation between Jesus and those who accuse him of exorcising in the power of Beelzebul, Luke, unlike Mark and Matthew, makes no reference to the Holy Breath as the source of Jesus' exorcisms. The reader will recall that in Mark's and Matthew's gospels Jesus claims to exorcise in the power of God's Breath. Luke's Jesus claims to do so by "the finger of God" (Lk 12:10).

Both versions of Jesus' reply to his accusers enjoy historical plausibility. Luke's version is, however, charged with irony. In the book of Exodus Pharaoh's magicians recognized that Moses and Aaron performed their miracles "by the finger of God" (Ex 8:15-19). In Luke's mind, these pagans possessed more insight and discernment than Jesus' Jewish adversaries.

Luke's account of this incident contrasts with those of Matthew and of Mark in yet another way. The latter two evangelists portray Jesus as warning his adversaries that in making their slanderous accusation they blaspheme God's Breath (Mk 3:28-29, Mt 12:30-32). Luke situates Jesus' warning against Breath blasphemy in another context. In Luke's gospel Jesus instructs his followers on the way to conduct themselves during times of persecution. Their reverence for the Father must inspire them to suffer martyrdom, if need be; they must confess the Son fearlessly; and they must avoid the "unforgivable sin" of blaspheming the Holy Breath. Luke, then, equates "blaspheming the Breath" with the apostasy of the baptized Christian, rather than with equating the action of the Breath with that of the devil, as Mark and Matthew had (Lk 12:4-12).

IV. The Baptismal Breath in John.

The fourth gospel makes no reference to Jesus' baptism by John, but it does have the Baptist witness to the fact that the Holy Breath did in fact descend upon Jesus and that Jesus will baptize his followers with that same divine Breath (Jn 1:29-34). It seems historically implausible that the Baptist would have shared personally in Jesus' experience of messianic commissioning. The Baptist's claim, then, to have seen the Breath's descent upon Jesus probably reflects more the special role assigned him in the fourth gospel: namely, that of witnessing to Jesus (Jn 1:6-8).

Moreover, in what may be a theological gloss on the Baptist's final testimony to Jesus, the fourth evangelist explains the reason why Jesus and not John enjoys the power to baptize with a sanctifying Breath: namely, she abides with Jesus permanently and dwells in him "without measure" (Jn 3:31-36). How should one interpret the meaning of this assertion? Does the Father give to the Son a measureless portion of the divine Breath, or does the Son pour her forth in measureless abundance? The fourth evangelist could have intended both interpretations and probably did. Jesus alone in virtue of his heavenly origin and unique dignity as Son of God has access to the divine Breath in measureless abundance as both her vessel and wellspring. As a consequence, the Breath of God dwells in Jesus as an inexhaustible source of life: she inspires his testimony to God, and consent to that testimony opens the gateway to eternal life (Jn 3:5-8).

Indeed, the fourth gospel portrays Breath-baptism itself as rebirth unto eternal life. In a private conversation with the Pharisee Nicodemus, Jesus assures him that only rebirth in water and Breath introduces one into the kingdom of God. That rebirth differs from being born of the flesh, because only the Breath of God can communicate "Breath" to mortals. Jesus portrays the process of rebirth as mysterious: like the wind, one cannot tell where the new birth comes from or where finally it will lead; but rebirth in the Breath gives a present share in the very life of God (Jn 8:21-34).

In speaking to Nicodemus Jesus distinguishes between "the Holy Breath" and "Breath." When preceded by the article "the" the Greek term for "Breath" in John's gospel designates the third member of the trinity, the Holy Breath whom Jesus will send. When in John's gospel the Greek term for "Breath" lacks an article, it designates the very life of God which the Father, the Son, and the Breath share. Moreover, for the fourth evangelist, the Holy Breath acting in Christian baptism conceives this same divine life in those who believe in Jesus.

In addition to attributing Breath-baptism to the action of the Holy Breath, the fourth evangelist portrays her as living water, as the inspiration of authentic Christian worship, and as a divine witness to Jesus. Let us probe in more detail the implications of each of these affirmations.

The Living Water.

In John's gospel the first mention of living water occurs in the course of Jesus' conversation with the Samaritan woman at Jacob's well. When the woman in unsettled by having a Jewish man request a drink from her, Jesus reassures her by stating: "If you knew the gift of God and who it is that is saying to you, 'Give me a drink,' you would have asked him, and he would have given you living water" (Jn 4:10).

Unlike the poisonous, saline waters of the Dead Sea, living water flows and gives life to plants, animals, and humans. Jesus, however, offers a living water that will slake human thirst for life after death. A mysterious gift, it will well up spontaneously in those who receive it.

Moreover, in calling this living water "the gift of God," Jesus assimilates it to both the Torah and to divine wisdom. Rabbinic literature refers to the law as God's gift; and divine wisdom, as we have seen in the preceding chapter, descends from on high as God's free and gratuitous gift. In the fourth gospel, however, Jesus himself communicates to those who ask him this mysterious gift of living water. His gift enlightens and teaches both divine wisdom and the obedience to God's will that wisdom inspires.

Not until late in Jesus' ministry, however, does the fourth evangelist reveal the true character of this living water. On the last day of the feast of Tabernacles, as the conflict between Jesus and his adversaries reaches a new intensity of bitterness, Jesus proclaims in the temple: "If any one thirst, let him come to me and drink. He who believes in me, as the scripture has said: 'Out of his heart shall flow rivers of living water'" (Jn 7:37-39).

In citing scripture, Jesus does not quote directly but seems to allude to passages in the Hebrew Bible which speak of drinking in the wisdom of God. Once again, therefore, the fourth evangelist speaks of the living water as a source of divine wisdom; but this time he also identifies the living water as the Holy Breath with which Jesus will baptize his followers (Jn 7:39).

Moreover, John probably intends the ambiquity in Jesus' vague citation. In Jesus' promise that "from within him shall flow rivers of living water," the phrase "from within him" probably refers not only to Jesus himself, the source of the living water, but also to his disciple in whom the living water will well up spontaneously. The promise also recalls Jesus' earlier assurance to the Samaritan woman that the living water he will give will well up to eternal life (Jn 4:14). The evangelist now makes it clear, however, that Jesus cannot give the gift of living water to his followers until he rises from the dead in glory (Jn 7:19).

At the moment of Jesus' death, the promised outpouring of living water is foreshadowed by the sign of blood and water which flows from the pierced side of the crucified messiah (Jn 19:33-34). The soldier thrusts the lance into Jesus' side in order to ensure that he has died; but the thrust is followed by a sign of everlasting life.

The water flowing from Jesus' side recalls the prophecy of Ezekiel that a torrent of water would pour forth from the temple of God, a torrent that would purify a sinful land and make it bloom (Ez 47:1-12). The water flowing from the violated temple of Jesus' body prefigures the living water he will bestow when, risen in glory on Easter morning, he will breathe a sanctifying Breath into his disciples (Jn 20:19-23).

Moreover, alluding possibly to this passage in the fourth gospel, the first letter of John assures us that the Breath, the water, and the blood all give the same testimony. The Holy Breath testifies with the water by inspiring the baptismal faith of Christians. She testifies with the blood by inspiring both Jesus' act of self-immolation on the cross and Christian faith in the saving power of his death (1 Jn 5:5-8).

The Source of Christian Worship.

In his conversation with the Samaritan woman, not only does Jesus promise her the gift of living water, but he also assures her that a day is coming when true believers will worship God neither in Jerusalem nor on Mount Gerazim but in Breath and truth; for the God who is Breath desires to be worshipped in Breath and truth (Jn 4:23-24).

Once again in John's gosepl we encounter the term "Breath" without an article before it. As we have seen, the term designates the life which the three divine persons share with one another and with those who believe in Jesus. Authentic worship, therefore, expresses the life which Christians share with God.

Authentic worship also transpires "in truth." In the fourth gospel, truth consecrates and sanctifies those who assent to it (Jn 17:17-19). Jesus, divine wisdom incarnate, confronts his disciples as "the way, the truth, and the life," as the very reality of the Father made visible (Jn 14:6-9). Authentic worship, therefore, seeks the face of the Father who is revealed in the incarnate Word. It does so with a wisdom begotten from above by the divine Breath who suffuses those who believe with Breath, with the very life of the Godhead.

Ultimately, however, authentic worship of God culminates in eucharistic worship. In the bread-of-life discourse, Jesus promises his followers that he will give them his own eucharistic flesh and blood to eat and drink. When some of them doubt him, he rebukes their lack of faith, assuring them that his promise is both Breath and life. Those who cannot believe him live mired in the flesh; they ignore the Breath who alone gives life (Jn 6:60-71).

In his rebuke Jesus contrasts sharply the divine Breath's life-giving potency and the impotence of "the flesh" when the latter resists her animating inspirations. Those, he warns, who cannot believe in his eucharistic presence ignore his divine origin (Jn 6:61-62). Their lack of faith only manifests that they themselves have not been reborn with the life which the Breath of God imparts. Lacking a share in Breath, in the divine life which the Holy Breath imparts, they cannot recognize Jesus' promise of the bread of life as an incarnation of Breath.

The Witness to Jesus.

Finally, in his last discourse to his disciples, John's Jesus promises several times that he will send them another witness like himself (Jn 14:16). This second witness will prolong Jesus' ministry in space and time by inspiring the witness of his disciples. The new witness will, therefore, instruct the disciples as Jesus himself had done and will inspire their confession of him in a way that conforms it to his own confession of the Father.

Jesus identifies the witness as "the Breath of truth" he will send from his Father, as the Holy Breath with which he will baptize his followers. As witness to Jesus she will speak for him, exhort his followers, and inspire their testimony to him. She will dwell in the disciples as she dwelt in Jesus. She will do battle for the divine truth incarnate in Jesus (Jn 14:16-17).

This witness proceeds from both Jesus and the Father (Jn 14:26, 16:7). The Father sends her at Jesus' intercession and in Jesus' name; but Jesus himself also sends her efficaciously (Jn 14:16, 26, 16:7). Indeed, the fact that both Father and Son send the witness simultaneously reveals their intimate union with one another (Jn 10:30).

As witness the Breath will abide with the disciples forever (Jn 14:16). As a consequence, they will know her immediately and intimately; for her indwelling will reveal her life-giving presence. She will make Christ himself present in his disciples (Jn 14:17-18).

The witness will teach the disciples "all things" and will "remind" them of Jesus' own instruction. Through her illumination, the disciples will appropriate Jesus' teachings with a new insight into their meaning. Indeed, they must await her coming to bear the full burden of the wisdom she imparts. Jesus' own departure from his followers in consequence of his death and glorification, therefore, far from seeking to cause them dismay only prepares the witness's empowering arrival. As the Breath of Jesus, she will teach only those things she hears from him as he has taught only what he has received from the Father (Jn 16:5-19).

Besides testifying to Jesus, the witness will also announce to the disciples "the things to come." She will unfold for them the future God has prepared: not just events within history but also eternal life with the risen and victorious Christ (Jn 16:13).

Nevertheless, in consequence of their witness to Jesus, his disciples will be drawn inexorably into his passion. "The world" will no more heed them than it listened to him. Expelled from synagogues, murdered by pious hypocrites who will profess their crime an act of divine homage, Jesus' disciples, through the action of the witness within them, will confess him fearlessly, even though some in their weakness will fall away from the truth (Jn 15:20-21, 16:1-2).

Nevertheless, through her action in Jesus' disciples the witness will pass judgment on the world's error. She will unmask the world's hypocritical piety and reveal its true sinfulness by dramatizing its lack of faith in God's incarnate Word. She will vindicate Jesus despite his crucifixion and death by manifesting his presence with the Father. In the process she will reverse the unjust judgment of condemnation passed by the world on Jesus and his followers. She will do so by revealing God's own condemnation of the demonic prince of this world who inspires the persecution of God's holy ones (Jn 16:7-15).

V. The Gospel Witness to God's Holy Breath.

An examination of the four gospels and their witness to the Holy Breath's action in Jesus reveals, then, important areas of agreement, convergence, and complementarity. As we have seen, the three synoptic gospels endorse fundamentally the same interpretation of Jesus' baptism. They link the descent of God's Breath upon him at the Jordan to his messianic commissioning by the Father. They see in this event eschatological significance: it manifests the dawning of the last age of salvation, although Luke underplays this aspect of Jesus' baptism. All three synoptics assert that the divine Breath comes to Jesus to reveal him as God's beloved Son and the beginning of a new Israel. She comes too to empower his messianic ministry in the image of the suffering servant of God. Although Mark especially of the three synoptic gospels insists most strongly on the fact that the divine Breath present in Jesus sets him in opposition to the forces of evil in this world, Matthew and Luke concur in this belief.

The fourth gospel makes no mention of Jesus' baptism but develops in more detail than the synoptics do the theological significance of her action in him. She abides in him in eschatological abundance thus revealing him as the presence and wellspring of eternal life. John also advances beyond the synoptics in portraying Breath-baptism as a mysterious rebirth. It communicates "Breath" to the baptized, a share in the eternal life of God.

All four gospels also agree that Breath-baptism sets the disciples of Jesus in opposition to the same forces of sin, darkness, and oppression as crucified the Christ. The fourth gospel, however, develops this synoptic insight in greater theological detail when it portrays the Holy Breath as the witness to the risen Lord who inspires Jesus' disciples' witness to him under persecution.

As we have seen, the synoptic gospels offer different interpretations of what it means to blaspheme the Breath. Matthew and Mark interpret it as mistaking her action for the work of demons; Luke presents Breath-blasphemy as the apostasy of the baptized Christian in the face of persecution. The first interpretation rather than Luke's probably expresses Jesus' own understanding of Breath-blasphemy.

In portraying the Holy Breath as living water, John's gospel links the action of the Holy Breath explicitly to the Christian's share in the resurrection of Jesus in ways that go beyond anything we find in the synoptic gospels. John also insists more clearly than the other three evangelists that the baptismal Breath inspires authentic eucharistic worship and belief in Jesus' real eucharistic presence. In addition, John links the action of the Holy Breath more explicitly to doctrinal orthodoxy: she inspires faith in the divine truth incarnate in Jesus and in his redemptive death.

The synoptic tradition, on the other hand, insists, as it develops, more explicitly on the moral consequences of

Breath-baptism. The Holy Breath comes not only to inspire the disciples' witness to Jesus even under persecution but also to teach them how to live in his image by accepting the practical demands of discipleship. She comes to free Christians to share their physical possessions with one another as an expression of their faith in God's providential care for them. She comes to create an open-ended community of faith which reaches out to sinners, the marginal, and the oppressed, a community concerned to share its goods with others on the basis of need and not of merit only, a community committed by preference to care for the poor. She comes to authenticate Christian worship by teaching Jesus' disciples to forgive one another with the same divine atoning love as he embodied.

Finally, all the gospels agree that the Holy Breath comes to Jesus not as an individual but in order that he might impart her to others and in the process create the church. In the chapter which follows we will examine in greater detail the divine Breath's action in the Christian community.

3

God Breathes on the Church

We have reflected in the two preceding chapters on how the action of God's Holy Breath in Israel culminated in Her inspiration of Jesus' religious vision and public ministry. All four gospels make it clear, however, that the Breath of God came to Jesus in order to transform him into the beginning of a new Israel. He brought the new Israel into being in part by his own preaching and example but also and especially by baptizing his followers with his own divine Breath.

The time has come, then, to examine the way in which the Holy Breath of Jesus acts within the church he founded. Our reflections divide into five parts. The first part examines the testimony of Paul the apostle to the divine Breath's action in his own apostolic ministry and in the communities he served. The second part of this chapter reflects on Luke the evangelist's narrative of the ways in which the Breath of Jesus created the church and directed its expansion. Section three probes some of the historical forces that have contributed to the decline among Christians of a living faith in the Holy Breath and in her charismatic inspirations. Part four describes the official Catholic rediscovery of the Breath's charisms which occurred at Vatican II and examines the popular re-appropriation of the gifts which occurred in the wake of the council. Finally, part five will ponder the ways in which sharing the Holy Breath's charismatic inspirations creates the shared faith of the church.

I. The Breath of the Risen Christ in the Letters of Paul.

The letters of Paul the apostle to the churches he founded and visited provide us with the earliest Christian documents we possess. In them we also discover first-hand evidence of the way in which the first Christians experienced the Breath of Christ. Moreover, in the letters of Paul we can also hear one of the apostles who saw the risen Jesus testify personally to the significance of that experience.

In point of fact Paul links intimately the resurrection of Jesus to the presence and activity of His Breath in the Christian community. For example, in the first letter to the Corinthians Paul describes Jesus' resurrection as his spiritualization. More specifically, Paul insists that the risen Christ confronts believers as the new Adam who re-founds the human race because by rising from the dead Jesus became "a life-giving Breath" (1 Cor 15:45).

In the second letter to the Corinthians Paul makes a similar affirmation. There Paul identifies the risen Christ with the Breath he sends to believers. Paul states baldly: "The Lord is the Breath" (2 Cor 3:17). Paul's statement occurs within an extended allegory. In it the apostle contrasts the imperishable glory of the new covenant with the fading glory of the covenant given at Sinai. After receiving the covenant from God on Mount Sinai, Paul contends, Moses' face so shone with a divine glory that he had to veil his countenance in the presence of the chosen people until that glory had finally faded. By contrast, the glory in the face of the risen Christ never fades. In Christ, moreover, God abrogated the covenant he made at Sinai; but the new covenant sealed in Christ lasts forever. The glory that shone on the face of Moses did not effect the justification of those who saw it. Those, however, who know the glory of the risen Christ are justified by sharing in the same divine Breath that animates him (2 Cor 3:7-18).

Paul's intent in identifying the Lord with the Breath has vexed scripture scholars, who have proposed at least six different interpretations of this statement. In Paul's letters the term "Lord" is generally reserved for the risen Christ; but some Pauline interpreters have suggested that when Paul says "The Lord is the Breath," the term "the Lord" refers to God the Father or to the Lord of the exodus. Most exegetes, however, agree that "the Lord" refers here also to the risen Christ; but they offer a variety of interpretations of what Paul means by the term "the Breath."

If, however, we read Paul's statement in second Corinthians in the light of his insistence in his first letter to that church that the resurrection spiritualized Jesus totally not only by giving him a mysterious pneumatic body but also by transforming him into a life-giving Breath, then the apostle's intention in equating the Lord and the Breath becomes clear enough.

Paul is insisting that the new covenent has been sealed through the resurrection of Jesus, for the risen Lord seals it in the hearts of believers through the empowering illumination of his Breath. Indeed, Jesus' resurrection brought the divine Breath's action in him to its culmination. It transformed him in her so totally that risen life now overflows from him to all who under her inspiration confess him as Lord.

In asserting, then, that "the Lord is the Breath," Paul is insisting that the risen Lord who breathes her into the church acts wherever she acts. Indeed her action makes the Lord present within his people. In other words, while the people of the old covenant perceived the divine Breath as the presence of God, Paul now perceives her as the presence of the risen Lord. In equating the Lord and the Breath, however, Paul intends to assert much more than their divine co-action; for the Breath gives us a present share in the glory of the risen Christ. Those who share the Breath of Christ live with imperishable, risen life. In addition, then, to enjoying a functional identity through their co-action in the Christian community, the risen Lord and his Breath share a vital identity, an identity of divine life that makes them one. That vital identity explains why those who share the Breath of the risen Lord share risen life itself.

In Paul's letters the term "flesh" designates the whole human person as earth-bound, death-bound, and sinful (Gal 5:13-26). Those, however, who share in the Breath of Jesus have a "down-payment" on their own resurrection (1 Cor 1:21-22). Not only does she inspire Christian hope in a universal resurrection (Rom 8:18-27); but her presence begins in us the same process of graced transformation that in Jesus culminated in his bodily resurrection (Rom 8:11).

We stand here at the heart of Paul's theology of the divine Breath. Let us begin to probe its implications.

Access to the Breath of Christ.

Paul seems never to have tired of testifying to the difference which the encounter with the risen Christ had made in his life. It had converted him from a persecutor of Christians into a witness to the truth of the gospel. Paul traced his authority as an apostle back to the Father and to the risen Lord; but Paul also insisted that the Breath of Jesus animated and sanctioned his apostolic witness (Rom 15:14-21, 1 Cor 1:1, 7:40, 12:28, Gal 1:11-2:21).

Paul saw the divine Breath sanctioning and sustaining his witness to the risen Christ by effecting in those to whom he preached a religious conversion analogous to the one he himself had experienced in his encounter with the risen Lord (1 Thess 1:4-6, 1 Cor 2:4-16, Phil 1:19). She inspired justifying faith in those who believed his apostolic witness (1 Cor 12:1-3), just as she worked their ongoing sanctification (1 Cor 6:9-11).

Moreover, a careful reading of the moral exhortation which closes the letter to the Romans makes it clear that Paul measured Christian holiness by willingness to submit to the ethics of discipleship which Jesus lived and proclaimed. Paul begins that exhortation by urging the Romans to transformation in the "renewal of your mind" which the Breath of Jesus effects in those who believe (Rom 8:1-39, 12:1-2). As Jesus had required of his followers, those renewed in mind share their possessions with one another in community. They do so on the basis of need and not of merit only. Such sharing must express mutual forgiveness and reconciliation in Christ's name. Christians must extend the same atoning love even to their enemies, for the gospel seeks to unite those whom sin has divided. In their special concern for the poor, Christians, should, moreover, extend to them real friendship, not class condescension (Rom 12:3-8, 9-21, 13:8-10).

Besides endorsing Jesus' moral teaching, Paul reflects in his letters on the religious significance of responding to the divine Breath's sanctifying enlightenment. She inspires Christian hope, faith, love, joy, peace, patience, kindness, goodness, faithfulness, gentleness, and self-control. Because Jesus' Breath imparts a spontaneous desire to live in his image, the Christian experiences her as the law that governs Christian conduct. Instead of being imposed extrinsically, however, as the law given at Sinai was, the rejuvenating enlightenment of Jesus' Breath fixes the mind and heart in freedom upon the things of God (Gal 5:5-6, 13-26, Rom 5:1-5, 8:1-13, 2 Cor 3:4-18). Indeed, the Breath's sanctifying presence transforms Christians individually and collectively into the living temple of God (1 Cor 3:16-17, 6:19-20).

Not only does Paul reflect theologically on the religious significance of responding to the Breath's sanctifying illuminations, but his vision of Christian morality actually advances beyond the moral teachings of Jesus on one important point. Paul realizes that now that Christ has risen and sent his Breath into the church, Christians need to share not only the physical supports of life but the Holy Breath's charismatic inspirations as well (Rom 12:3-8).

The term "charism" means gift. It derives from the Greek word "charis," which means gift or grace. Charisms particularize the divine gift made to us in the death and glorification of Jesus and in the sending of His Breath into the world. Charisms particularize the grace of God by teaching Christians to embody the Christ-like love they have for one another in concrete acts of service both to individuals and to the community as a whole.

Sharing the charisms transforms the church into the body of Christ, as each member contributes something to its shared life. Some give an outstanding example of faith. Others pray in tongues or speak messages in tongues. Others still interpret tongues. Prophets summon the community to respond to the challenge of gospel living. Some teachers proclaim the divine wisdom incarnate in Jesus; others instruct the community in other ways. Some serve as instruments of divine healing, even of miraculous healing. Discerners sanction the Breath's genuine inspirations and unmask unauthentic religious impulses. The Breath calls some to celibacy, others to marriage. Apostles, administrators, and church officials bear the burden of pastoral leadership with the assistance of helpers, of deacons, of those who supervise the distribution of alms, and of those who serve the needy (1 Cor 12-14, Rom 12:6-8).

Paul commonly invoked four criteria in judging the authenticity of any of the Breath's gifts of service: order, reciprocity, union, and faith. The principle of order demands respect for social propriety, due process, and legitimate authority (1 Cor 5:3-5, 12:27-28, 14:26-40). The principle of reciprocity requires openness to the Breath's action in every member of the church, on the one hand, and respect for the consciences of others, on the other (1 Cor 12:14-26). The principle of union rejects as unauthentic any claim to charismatic inspiration which violates the bond of love uniting Christians to God and to one another (1 Cor 12:12-13:13, Rom 5:1-5). The principle of faith requires that service conform to sound doctrine (1 Cor 12:1-3).

II. Pentecost.

The letters of Paul give a good insight into the way in which the first Christians experienced the Breath of Jesus on a day-to-day basis. In the Acts of the Apostles, Luke tells the story of her arrival on Pentecost and of the way she presided over the spread of the gospel from Jerusalem to Rome.

At the beginning of Acts the risen Christ repeats and clarifies a promise which he had made at the end of Luke's gospel (Lk 24:49). He assures the assembled disciples that they will receive power when the Holy Breath comes upon them in Jerusalem, for she will empower them to witness to him even to the ends of the earth (Acts 1:8). Breath-baptism will, then, effect the universal proclamation of Christ.

On Pentecost the Breath arrives under the double sign of wind and of fire, the same signs which had accompanied the prophet Elijah's ascension into heaven (2 Kings 2:9-15). That event had revealed to the prophet Elisha that he would receive a privileged "double portion" of his master's prophetic Breath. On Pentecost, however, the Breath comes as the Breath of Jesus, not of Elijah. She comes, moreover, not to a single individual, but in eschatological abundance: she is poured out by God on "all flesh" in fulfillment of Joel's prophecy (Acts 2:14-22, Joel 3:1-5).

The Pentecostal fire also recalls the Baptist's prophecy that Jesus would one day baptize his followers with a Breath of purification and of judgment. She comes, however, in "tongues like fire" in order to effect that purification and judgment in the universal proclamation of the gospel (Acts 2:3).

The universal proclamation of Christ is also foreshadowed by the eruption of glossolatic speech among the disciples gathered in the upper room (Acts 2:4). Luke interprets the appearance of glossolalia[1] as a sign of the gathering

[1]The gift of tongues is sometimes referred to as "glossolalia." Those who erroneously defend the literal truth of everything in the Bible tend to interpret tongue-speaking, or glossolalia, as in every instance the speaking of a foreign language. They tend to justify this interpretation by an appeal to the "miracle of tongues" recorded in the second chapter of the Acts of the Apostles, the only text in Acts in which glossolalia is associated with communicating in a foreign tongue. Contemporary linguistic studies of glossolalia, however, discover in tongue-speaking, not the miraculous speaking of a foreign language, but the uttering of language-like sounds without vocabulary, grammar, or syntax. [Cf. William J. Samarin, *Tongues of Men and Angels* (New York: Macmillan, 1972).] Moreover, contemporary exegesis of Acts 2 discovers there, not the factual narration of a miracle, but a theological reflection on the significance of the Breath's arrival on Pentecost. [See, for example: George Montague, "Baptism in the Spirit and Speaking in Tongues: A Biblical Appraisal," *Theology Digest,* XXI (Winter, 1973), 373ff.]

of Israel from the four corners of the earth (Acts 2:5-13), an event that prepares in turn the Breath's outpouring on all humankind (Acts 2:14-21).

In linking Joel's prophecy of universal salvation to glossolalia, Luke may also have intended to portray Pentecost as a reversal of Babel. At Babel, God had confounded every human tongue as a sign of the race's sinfulness (Gen 11:1-9); now he does it anew as a portent of universal salvation. Most certainly, however, Luke desired to portray Pentecost as the fulfillment of the Baptist's prophecy that Jesus would baptize his followers with a Holy Breath and fire (Acts 2:37-39). Moreover, the Breath of Jesus on her arrival immediately creates the church of Jesus by teaching his disciples obedience to the ethics of discipleship which he lived and proclaimed (Acts 4:32-5:11).

Luke's account of the Breath's arrival on Pentecost contrasts with the account of her sending which ends the fourth gospel. At the end of John's gospel Jesus appears to his disciples on Easter day, not on Pentecost, breathes on them, and imparts to them a sanctifying Breath with the assurance: "If you forgive the sins of any they are forgiven; if you retain the sins of any, they are retained" (Jn 20:19-23). As in Matthew and Luke the Breath in John proceeds from Jesus in both purification and judgment. She purifies sinners who open their hearts to her in faith; she judges the hard-hearted and unrepentant.

In portraying the risen Christ breathing his commissioning Breath into his disciples, John links her arrival theologically

The gift of tongues is, therefore, best interpreted as fundamentally a gift of prayer in which, through the utterance or singing of language-like sounds, one gives verbal expression to a felt, pre-conceptual openness to God. Similarly, one who utters a "message in tongues" in the context of contemporary charismatic prayer speaks aloud to a worshipping community as though uttering a message in grammar and syntax, even though the individual in fact speaks sounds devoid of both. One who interprets such a message does not translate its meaning but instead speaks some word to the gathered community which the "message in tongues" has prepared the community to hear. [Cf. Donald L. Gelpi, S.J., *Charism and Sacrament: A Theology of Christian Conversion* (New York: Paulist, 1976) 72-80.]

with Easter and with the event of the resurrection. Luke dates her arrival with Pentecost, after the apparitions of the risen Christ have ceased. Both John and Luke, of course, are writing a theological reflection on the significance of the Breath's arrival, not a newspaper account of that event. They therefore tell the story of how she came in different ways in order to make different but legitimate theological points.

Both evangelists, however, may also be stating a literal truth about the Breath's arrival in the Christian community. Those who saw the risen Christ would certainly have experienced a personal religious enlightenment which they would have ascribed to the Breath of God. Even so, her arrival on Pentecost to create the church through her sanctifying, charismatic inspirations might well have happened after the apparitions of the risen one had ceased. In other words, the risen Lord may have poured her out upon his disciples in stages, first on those who saw him, then upon the community as a whole.

The Breath of Christ and the Spread of the Gospel.

As in the letters of Paul, however, in Acts the Breath of Jesus also unites the Christian community into a church by an outpouring of her charisms of service: tongues, prophecy, cures and exorcisms, preaching, works of mercy (Acts 2:1, 3:6, 4:7-12, 30, 19:46, 16:18, 19:6). She especially confirms the apostolic witness to Christ with signs and wonders (Acts 2:43, 5:12-16, 14:13, 15:12). She empowers Peter and the other apostles to confront boldly the same powers that crucified Jesus (Acts 4:23-31).

She thwarts every attempt to suppress the gospel by transforming persecution into an occasion for the church's spread. As a consequence of the persecution of the Jerusalem church which follows the stoning of Stephen, for example, the deacon Philip begins the conversion of the Samaritans and baptizes an Ethiopian eunuch (Acts 8:4-40). The latter event foreshadows the conversion of the gentiles, which Paul, that relentless persecutor of Christians, will effect after his own conversion to Christ (Acts 9:1-19).

The Holy Breath also presides over the gentile mission which Paul and Barnabas conduct. She sets them aside to evangelize Asia Minor (Acts 3:12). In the council of Jerusalem she sanctions their practice of baptizing uncircumcised gentiles (Acts 15:5-29). She then sends Paul off again on his second missionary journey. She prevents him from going to Bythinia (Acts 16:7). At Troas Paul is called by a vision to Macedonia (Acts 16:9). She descends dramatically on the disciples of John the Baptist whom Paul baptizes at Ephesus (Acts 19:1-7). She confirms the whole of Paul's ministry with abudant signs of healing and deliverance (Acts 19:11-12).

As Jesus had predicted in Luke's gospel, however, the Breath-filled apostle is drawn inexorably into Jesus' own passion. Repeatedly harassed and imprisoned by the enemies of the gospel, he is flogged at Philippi (Acts 16:22). As Paul returns to Jerusalem for the last time, the Holy Breath inspires repeated prophecies that warn him to expect imprisonment and persecution in the Holy City (Acts 20:22-23, 21:11-14). She thwarts the malice of Paul's adversaries, however, by using his very imprisonment by the Roman authorities as the occasion of his transportation to Rome, where he proclaims Christ in the symbolic heart and center of the gentile world of the first century (Acts 28:30-31).

In making his last farewell to the disciples at Ephesus before his final return to Jerusalem, Paul commends the community to the elders which the divine Breath has constituted over-seers of God's flock (Acts 20:28). The scene foreshadows the end of the apostolic era but simultaneously gives the assurance that despite the death of the apostles the Breath of Jesus will continue to preside over the spread of the gospel.

III. The Eclipse of the Breath-Consciousness.

An examination of the New Testament witness to the

divine Breath makes it clear that the first Christians experienced her activity in a variety of ways: she graciously transformed each individual Christian, she created the church, and she directed the universal proclamation of the risen Christ. Let us reflect briefly on each of these activities in turn.

The Holy Breath transforms each Christian personally. She effects in them conversion and justifying faith in the risen Christ. She seals and regenerates every member of the church in the one baptism that unites them to God and to one another (Eph 4:5, 30-32, Tit 3:4-7). She comes to transform each believer in the image of Jesus. She teaches each of the faithful to put on Jesus' mind by obeying the ethics of discipleship he lived and proclaimed. In the process she transforms every Christian into God's adopted child (Eph 1:3). She dwells in Christians as a source of personal power and strength (Eph 3:14-19), as she teaches them to battle the powers of evil with the sword of her divine word (Eph 5:17).

In addition to effecting the personal justification and sanctification of every Christian, the Holy Breath also builds them up into the church, the living body of Christ. This she does in two ways: (1) by bringing into existence a community of faith sharing which cares for each of its members, especially those most in need and (2) by making Christian love practical in charismatically inspired deeds of service. She inspires the church's shared worship, transforming it into a jubilant spiritual intoxication (Col 1:8).

Finally, the divine Breath inspires the universal proclamation of the gospel: both the personal witness of individuals and the collective witness of the church. In the process she advances the conversion of all people to Christ and the Christianization of human society.

The letters of Paul and the Acts of the Apostles give solid evidence that sharing the charisms of God's Breath contributed significantly to Breath-consciousness among the first Christians. Nevertheless, in the fifth century we find Augustine of Hippo suggesting that the Breath's charisms were intended only for the first generation of believers. Augustine's suggestion reflects the serious eclipse of Breath consciousness that had occurred in the centuries that separated him from the apostolic church. What had happened?

We can point with some confidence to two historical forces that helped motivate the eclipse of Breath consciousness: theological confusion concerning her role in salvation history and the disappearance of the catechumenate. Let us reflect on each of these forces in turn.

Throughout the Bible, the Breath of God is perceived as the source of every kind of religious enlightenment. In the third century, however, some influential theologians began to attribute graced enlightenment, not to the Breath of God, but to the divine Word. In other words, these theologicans began attributing to the second person of the trinity all the saving, redemptive acts which the Bible attributes to the third.

These theologians acted in good faith; but as we look back on their work from a contemporary perspective, we have reason to question the speculative moves they made. They conflated illegitimately ideas derived from Greek philosophy with New Testament concepts. In the philosophy of middle Platonism they found the notion that the eternal ideas that give intelligibility to all reality reside in a divine intelligence called in Greek a *logos*. The philosophical term *"logos"* meant rule, pattern, or word. In middle Platonism the divine *logos* functioned as the source of all rational enlightenment.

In John's gospel these same Christian theologians found Jesus proclaimed as the Word *(Logos)* of God (Jn 1:1). They assumed, wrongly, that when John called Jesus "the word of God" he meant the same thing as the philosophers of middle Platonism meant by the divine intelligence they called a *logos*. Accordingly, these theologians began to speak of the second person of the trinity not only as the source of all rational enlightenment but also as the origin of all graced enlightenment as well. Having done so, they could no longer explain what role the divine Breath performs within the history of salvation.

Not all the fathers of the church endorsed this understanding of the *Logos.* Some, like Irenaeus of Lyons, who flourished in the second century, and Victorinus, who flourished in the fourth, interpreted the second person of the trinity as the spoken word of God, both as the one who makes God visible to us by his incarnation and as the person in God through whom the Father and the Breath act to save us. This second group of church fathers continued to speak of the divine Breath as the wisdom of God and source of all gracious enlightenment; but they had much less influence than those who attributed graced illumination to the Son rather than to the divine Breath. Moreover, to this day theological thinking, especially in the west, focuses narrowly on the second person of the trinity to the neglect of the first and of the third.

In addition to theological confusion concerning the Holy Breath's role within salvation history, a second force probably contributed to the eclipse of Breath-consciousness: namely, the decline of the catechumenate. During the first three centuries of the Christian era, the church took great pains to ensure that prior to their sacramental initiation converts had indeed not only experienced an initial conversion to Christ but had made significant strides in personal holiness and in their willingness to serve others under the divine Breath's guidance. Those preparing for the rites of initiation were called catechumens: that is to say, people still being catechized, or instructed, in the faith.

In the fourth century, Christianity became, first, one of the official religions of the Roman empire, then, the only officially recognized religious faith. As Christianity became socially fashionable through imperial patronage, more and more people presented themselves for baptism, but they chafed under the rigors of the catechumenate. In larger and larger numbers people were admitted to the sacraments who showed minimal, if any, signs of genuine conversion. By the fifth century, the catechumenate had disappeared. The religious mediocrity which its disappearance symbolized almost certainly contributed to the general eclipse of Breath-consciousness among Christians.

Although we discover an abortive theological interest in the charisms of the divine Breath during the thirteenth century, the piety of most Catholics during the middle ages did not qualify as charismatic in any visible sense. During the Reformation both Catholics and Protestants tended to assume that Augustine had had the right of it. The charisms had been intended only for first generation Christians. In fact anyone who aspired to charismatic piety incurred censure and suspicion and was regarded as the self-deluded victim of spiritual pride.

The Charisms Rediscovered.

By the nineteenth century, Breath-consciousness in the western church had degenerated to the point that theologians began speaking of the third person of the trinity as the forgotten God; but some of them began a scholarly retrieval of her place within Christian piety. An initial wave of research bore fruit in Pope Leo XIII's encyclical on the Holy Spirit, *Divinum illud munus* (1897).[2] The letter summarized important medieval insights into the reality of the Holy Breath but did little to spark popular devotion to the third person of the trinity.

A second wave of scholarly research inspired Pope Pius XII's encyclical on the mystical body of Christ, *Mystici corporis* (1943).[3] This second papal document popularized the Pauline doctrine that the Holy Breath animates the church and transforms it into the mystical body of Christ. It also called for further research into the Holy Breath's charismatic inspirations.

By the time Vatican II was convoked in 1962, theologians had reached a solid consensus that the divine Breath's charis-

[2]In English this document is commonly referred to as *The Encylical Letter of Pope Leo XIII on the Holy Spirit.*

[3]In English this document is normally referred to as *The Encyclical Letter of Pope Pius XII on the Mystical Body of Christ.*

matic inspirations offer the correct theological rubric for understanding the lay apostolate and lay spirituality. The bishops at the council endorsed this insight, rejected the idea that the charisms were intended only for first generation Christians, and called them instead a perennial endowment of the church. Indeed, Vatican II grounded the ministry of both the clergy and the laity in the divine Breath's charismatic promptings *(Lumen gentium,* 4, 7; *Apostolicam actuositatem*, 3; *Ad gentes*, 23, 28; *Presbyterorum ordinis*, 9).[4]

Pope John Paul II's recent encyclical on the Holy Breath *Dominum et vivificantem* has contributed significantly to papal teaching on the subject. This letter retrieves more systematically than any previous papal document New Testament teaching about the Breath of Jesus.[5]

This official doctrinal retrieval of faith in the divine Breath's present, charismatic inspirations would, however, probably have remained a dead letter had not the charismatic renewal transformed popular piety in the wake of the council. Blending the piety of the main-line churches with the piety of classical Pentecostalism, charismatic prayer gave many contemporary Christians the kind of vivid experience of the charisms which Paul the apostle and Luke the evangelist had described. Protestant Pentecostal churches had begun actively cultivating the charisms early in the twentieth century.

The charismatic renewal has, however, also unwittingly occasioned popular misunderstandings about the gifts as well. In learning about the charisms from Protestant Pentecostals, main-line Christians sometimes imbibed biblical fundamentalism as well. Moreover, the very existence of a

[4]These conciliar documents are often given the following titles in English: *Lumen gentium:* The Dogmatic Constitution on the Church; *Apostolicam actuositatem,* Decree on the Apostolate of the Laity; *Ad gentes,* Decree on the Church's Missionary Activity; *Presbyterorum ordinis,* Decree on the Ministry and Life of Priests.

[5]In English this document is normally referred to as *The Encyclical Letter of Pope John Paul II on the Holy Spirit in the Church and in the World.* For an English translation of this encyclical see: *Origins: NC Documentary Service* (June 12, 1986), vol. 16, no. 4, 77-102.

particular movement within the church which calls itself (in obedience to a request by the North American Catholic bishops) "the charismatic renewal" has created the false impression that only Christians who attend prayer meetings deserve to be called charismatic. In point of fact, as Vatican II insists, every baptized Christian is called by God to live in openness to the Breath's charismatic empowering. Indeed, as we shall see in the section which follows, the very existence of the church's shared faith results directly from sharing all the Breath's charisms in community.

V. Charismatic Consciousness and Faith

In the course of this chapter we have reflected on the New Testament witness to the Holy Breath's action in the church, and we have examined some of the historical forces which led to the eclipse of Breath consciousness. We have also reflected both on the theological attempt to retrieve living faith in the Breath's inspirations which culminated in the teachings of Vatican II; and we have weighed the popular rediscovery of the charisms in contemporary piety. In the final section of this chapter we will attempt to understand the ways in which the divine Breath by her gracious illumination actually creates the church.

The disciples of Jesus became a church on Pentecost. When the promised Breath of Jesus finally arrived, she first worked in his disciples a conversion of heart. She transformed a group of timid, half-hearted followers into a prophetic community willing to risk suffering, persecution, and even death in their dedication to spreading the good news about Jesus.

Christian conversion begins in the heart, with a repentant confrontation with all those attitudes that divide one from God. The repentant face the fear, guilt, and resentment that rankles often half-consciously within them. They renounce all such sinful attitudes and claim for themselves the divine forgiveness revealed in God's incarnate Word.

In the dynamics of Christian conversion repentance gives way to a heart-felt consent in faith to the divine beauty incarnate in Jesus and in people whose lives resemble his. Commitment to Jesus brings with it the determination to live in his image and to allow his Breath to empower one to do so.

Moral transformation in Jesus' image completes the first dynamic of Christian conversion which repentance begins. The first dynamic, moreover, gives rise to a second: the ongoing graced transformation of the convert's natural and sinful habits. As the vision of the gospel transforms human aspirations, it gives rise to Christian hope for salvation in Christ. As that same vision changes our intuitive and rational perceptions of reality, it gives rise to the virtue of faith. As it informs the judgments of conscience it inspires the deeds of charity. In other words, the Breath of Jesus sanctifies us by teaching us through prayer and Christian practice to grow in hope, faith, and love. In this way she enables us to put on the mind and attitudes of Jesus himself.

Those baptized in the Breath of Christ dedicate their lives as he did to the work of the kingdom. They seek to bring into existence a community of religious faith whose trust in God's providential care frees it to share its possessions with others, especially with the neediest. The Breath-baptized seek to build a universal community that excludes no one in principle from its practical care and concern and that reaches out, as Jesus did, to the poor, the marginal, the outcast. They seek to build a community of worship and of faith whose members forgive one another with the atoning love of Christ. In other words, the fundamental dynamics of initial and ongoing conversion which the Holy Breath inspires creates with moral necessity the community of faith we call the church.

The Catholic church has traditionally and correctly taught that the church mediates the life of God to those who belong to it. A narrowly hierarchical view of the church portrays its ordained leaders as an exclusive channel of divine grace to lay Christians. Vatican II correctly rejected such a view of the church as false. In the vision of the council all the members of the church share in the Breath of Jesus. All mediate her to one another. They do so by growing in holiness and by serving one another in response to her charismatic inspirations.

Indeed, only by sharing all the Breath's charisms in community can Christians achieve anything like shared faith consciousness. Communities come to consciousness somewhat differently from individuals. Individuals grow in consciousness when they distinguish images, concepts, and realities from one another and then understand how those same images, ideas, and realities interrelate. Communities, however, come to shared consciousness as communities by a complex process of interpretation; for a community achieves consciousness as a community when its members share memories, hopes, and lives.

Shared consciousness results most immediately from the kinds of shared experiences that create families and friendships. The members of a large, historical, world-wide community like the church cannot, however, all share experiences with one another immediately and directly. Instead, such a large community comes to an initial shared cosciousness as a community when it owns the events which found it. The church for example, looks back to the life, death, and resurrection of Jesus and to Pentecost as the founding events that give it its Christian identity.

In order to own the events that found it, a community must reach a consensus in its understanding of how those events occurred and what they signify. Without agreement on both these points a community will fragment, as the church did at the time of the Reformation.

To the extent that any community reaches consensus about the significance both of the events which found it and of the history which links it to those events, to that extent such a community will share a corporate sense of identity. As Americans, for example, we share a national identity to the extent that we understand our own historical roots. As Christians, we share a corporate identity in faith by recalling the story of

Jesus and of the church he founded, as we do at every eucharist.

Shared memories help create shared consciousness in communities; but memory alone does not suffice. The members of a community also reach shared consciousness when on the basis of sound historical self-understanding they aspire to a shared future. Christians hope ultimately for union with God and with one another in Christ; but they also share shorter-term hopes and aspirations for the conversion of all people to the gospel and for the Christianization of human society. We shall return to this last point in the chapter which follows.

Shared memories and shared hopes lay the foundation for shared communal awareness; but only when all the members of a community also share their lives in practical ways do they come to full consciousness as communities. Not only, then, must a community mobilize the gifts of its members in order to recall its origins and agree on a common future; but it must also motivate its members to collaborate actively with one another in order to transform its shared hopes into actualities.

A community of faith like the church also achieves shared awareness by sharing its memories, hopes, and lives. Christians, however, must share their memories, hopes, and lives in faith if they hope to achieve shared consciousness as a community of faith.

The Christian community can come to shared faith consciousness only by charismatic openness to all the divine Breath's charismatic inspirations. By that I mean that the church forever needs prophets to call it to ongoing repentance and ever renewed hope in God. Shared gifts of prayer and of healing endow the church with a shared sense of God's presence. Shared prayer in tongues reminds the church of the Breath's arrival on the first Pentecost and teaches Christians to regard Pentecost as an ongoing historical event. If the church hopes to grow collectively in holiness, it will always need teachers of wisdom to guide it in its imitation of Christ, just as it will always need historians and other instructors to remind it of its graced and sinful history and to teach other things useful for its well-being. While the charisms of teaching nourish the church's shared memories in faith, its prophets challenge Christians to shared readiness for the future God is preparing for it. Discerners enable the community to distinguish the Breath's authentic inspirations from natural or sinful impulses. Pastoral leaders in the church, whether ordained or lay, mobilize the gifts of each of the members of the Christian community in an effort to transform that future into an actuality. Administrators facilitate group activities like instruction and the care of the poor. Sacramental ministers summon the church to shared acts of worship.

In this way, as each member of the community serves the others in charismatic responsiveness to the divine Breath's inspirations, the Christian community achieves shared consciousness in faith. It can do so in no other way; for the sharing of the charisms of service in commuinity creates a matrix of divine grace in which the young and neophytes can grow to Christian maturity. As that occurs, they grow in their own ability to minister charismatically to others and thus learn to assume greater and greater personal reponsibility for contributing to the church's shared faith consciousness.

All Christians are, then, called to charismatic openness to the Breath of Christ; and as Christians they live responsible before God to cultivate the kind of ongoing conversion and personal prayerfulness that will sensitize them to the divine Breath's sanctifying and charismatic inspirations. By the same token, those who fail to respond in any way to the Breath's charismatic inspirations to that extent diminish the church's shared faith consciousness.

In this chapter we have been reflecting on the ways in which the Holy Breath creates the church by her inspirations. In the chapter which follows we will examine how she presides over the conversion of all people to Christ and over the graced transformation of human society.

4

God Breathes on the World

In the course of the preceding chapter we have discovered two fundamental ways in which God's breathing shapes the faith experience of contemporary Christians. In chapter II we saw that the Breath of Jesus sanctifies those who believe in him by teaching them to put on his mind. This they do by submitting to the ethics of discipleship which he lived and proclaimed. In the preceding chapter we examined a second way in which God's Holy Breath enlightens contemporary Christians: she does so by dispensing her charisms. Through them she calls Christians to a mutual service in community that creates the church's shared faith awareness.

The divine Breath that descended like a rushing wind on the disciples gathered in the upper room on the first Pentecost did more, however, than bind them to one another in a community of shared faith and worship. She also sent them forth to witness publicly to Christ and to proclaim the good news to the ends of the earth. Indeed, in Luke's narrative of the events that created the church, the Holy Breath gathers the Christian community again and again for the very purpose of extending and empowering its missionary activity (Acts 2:1-3:26, 4:23-31, 11:1-21, 13:1-3, 15:5-35). Moreover, ever since the first Pentecost the same two forms of graced enlightenment which the Breath imparts to create the church—the sanctifying appropriation of the mind of Christ and the call to charismatic ministry—also inform the church's public, apostolic witness to the risen Christ.

In the present chapter we will examine how the Breath's inspirations empower the church's public, prophetic witness to the gospel. That witness includes two distinct but related forms of ministry: the conversion of all people to Christ and the graced transformation of human society. As we shall see, the success or failure of both of these ministries depends entirely on the willingness of contemporary Christians to allow the Breath of Jesus to teach them to put on his mind and to minister charismatically to the needs of human kind.

In the pages which follow we shall first examine the church's missionary apostolate: for God breathes on the world most obviously in the universal proclamation of Christ. Next we shall ponder the way in which the Breath of God seeks to grace the structures of human society. Here we shall reflect on the lay apostolate; for, as we shall see, the chief responsibility for serving as God's instruments in transforming the social world in which we live rests upon the laity. We shall, moreover, examine two different kinds of social structures which the Breath of God graces, principally through the witness of lay Christians. We shall ponder first the gracing of the family, which gives social structure to intimate human relations. Then we shall address the more complex challenges which larger, impersonal institutional structures like government and the economy pose to contemporary lay apostles.

I. The Missionary Church.

Missionary activity differs from ecumenical dialogue. The latter seeks to restore to one eucharistic communion Christians at present divided from one another. Missionary activity, by contrast, seeks to convert to Christ those who have never heard of him (*Ad gentes,* 6).

The second Vatican council teaches us, quite correctly, that every baptized Christian participates in the church's missionary apostolate; for every Christian is bound by the new covenant to witness to Christ through word and example. The council, therefore, calls upon all believers to take advantage of every opportunity offered them to win others to Christ (*Ad gentes,* 23); and it exhorts Christians to support the church's missionary apostolate with prayers and with generous financial contributions in proportion to their means (*Ad gentes,* 35-38).

Some Christians, however, experience a special vocation to proclaim the good news to non-Christians living in foreign lands. Only those whom the Breath of God anoints with appropriate gifts should aspire to such a vocation. It ranks, however, among the principal means which she employs in order to ensure that the gospel is proclaimed to every nation.

Every charism, including the charism of laboring as a foreign missionary, empowers one to minister to others in Jesus' name and in a specific manner. The Christian community correctly holds up to its missionaries high standards of virtue and professional competence. The church demands that missionaries possess nobility and generosity of heart, adaptability, sympathy, warmth, and responsiveness to persons and to their special needs. It also requires of missionaries depth of faith, prayer, self-sacrifice, and zeal for the gospel.

Vatican II teaches that the Breath's charisms ground the rights and duties of Christians within the church (*Apostolicam actuositatem,* 3).[1] Accordingly, those whom the Breath of Jesus calls to the missions have the duty to respond to that call, for it comes from God. At the same time, they also have the right to expect that the Christian community provide them with the means of deepening and developing their gift of service. Missionaries legitimately expect from the church sound professional training in theology, in foreign languages, in the history and culture of those to whom they are sent, in missiology, in catechetics, in communications, and in the other pastoral skills they will need in order to

[1] *Apostolicam actuositatem* is often referred to in English as the *Decree on the Apostolate of the Laity.*

minister effectively (*Ad gentes,* 23-27).

By calling individual Christians to the missionary apostolate the gift-giving Breath of Christ helps ensure the spread of the gospel and the church's establishment in non-Christian cultures. Pastoral experience in the missions teaches, however, that the effective evangelization of the nations requires more than the ministry of individual charismatic leaders, however important their contribution to the church's total missionary enterprise. The effective evangelization of mission territories requires the collective witness of communities of faith that embody the mind of Christ in their day-to-day living.

Vatican II's Decree on the Church's Missionary Activity, *Ad gentes,* makes this point clearly and unambiguously. This document distills into a few short chapters the pastoral wisdom of generations of Christian missionaries. It predicates the spread of the gospel on the willingness of Christian communities to embody the moral vision of Jesus in their dealings with Christian and non-Christian alike. Vatican II insists on the collective, ecclesial character of that lived, day-to-day witness. It calls for the creation of communities of thoroughly converted Christians whose collective living of the gospel creates a realm of grace and of healing capable of attracting new converts to Christ (*Ad gentes,* 10-22).

In other words, not only does the spread of the gospel require Christian evangelists charismatically anointed by God's Breath to proclaim Christ with power to those who do not know him, but it also demands the corporate witness of Christian communities whose openness to that same divine Breath bears fruit in their obedience to the moral demands of discipleship.

A sound insight into the ethics of discipleship which Jesus lived and proclaimed gives concrete moral shape to such a witness. Those who embody the mind of Christ live in communities whose faith motivates them to reach out to all who suffer need, Christian and non-Christian alike. Open hospitality and mutual forgiveness, therefore, play an important part in the church's missionary activity. So too does practical concern for the needy. Vatican II, for example, exhorts missionary communities to conduct a relentless war against famine, ignorance, and disease and to show special compassion to the poor, the marginal, and the outcast. The council summons communities imbued with missionary zeal to challenge the social, economic, and political injustices that oppress and degrade people (*Ad gentes,* 10-12). Christian communities which include both Christians and non-Christians within their compassionate concern serve as centers of evangelical outreach that proclaim the gospel in deed and not just in word alone. At the same time, the sharing of the Breath's charisms in such communities creates a matrix of shared faith within which to evangelize neophytes and to support the faith of recent converts.

II. The Challenge of the Lay Apostolate.

God breathes on the world in the zeal of Christian missionaries; but the evangelization of unbelievers does not exhaust the ways in which the Breath of Jesus saves the world from its own sinfulness. She also labors in the efforts of committed Christians to transform the structures of human society in the ways that the gospel demands.

All believers need to resist the forces of sin and unbelief at work in the world. Nevertheless, Vatican II places the chief responsibility for the graced transformation of secular society squarely on the shoulders of lay Christians. Let us try to understand why.

The lay apostolate derives its character from the state of life and of health of individual Christians, from their professional and social commitments, and from their charismatic gifts (*Apostolicam actuositatem,* 3-4, 10). Some lay apostles work full time in church-sponsored institutions; the vast majority, however, live and labor in a secular context. As a consequence, they ordinarily possess both better skills and greater opportunity than the ordained to influence the policies and decisions of secular society; and for that reason they bear the principal responsibility for effecting its graced transformation.

In its secular outreach, therefore, the lay apostolate seeks nothing less than the graced renewal of our social world. It goes without saying that the pace and complexity of modern life poses enormous challenges to those involved in such an apostolate. For example, the tensions that shape contemporary society place the family under enormous social pressure, breed racial conflict and other forms of discrimination, pit the rich nations against the poor, and ensnare the leaders of the eastern and western block in dangerous ideological conflicts that threaten the annihilation of all people in a nuclear holocaust (*Gaudium et spes.* 1-8).[2]

In the rest of this chapter we will examine four different fields of the lay apostolate: the family, the economy, politics, and international relations. The family gives institutional shape to intimate, interpersonal human relationships, while larger, more impersonal institutions structure economic, political, and international activity. In the course of our reflections we shall attempt to understand how God breathes on each of these corners of our social world.

As in our reflections on the church's missionary activity we will in approaching the lay apostolate examine two distinct but interrelated actions of God's Holy Breath: her sanctifying action and her charismatic inspirations. We shall discover that as the Breath of Jesus transforms human interpersonal relationships, she teaches his disciples to love others as Jesus did. In gracing impersonal social structures she imbues Christians with Jesus' passion for justice. Moreover, in both instances, she empowers believers charismatically to serve one another in the image of the Lord.

[2]*Gaudium et spes* is usually referred to in English as the *Pastoral Constitution on the Church in the Modern World.*

III. The Gracing of Marriage.

In this section we shall examine some of the ways in which the Breath of Christ heals, sanctifies, and transforms human interpersonal relationships. We shall do so by describing the graced transformation of marital love. We will first ponder some of the forces in contemporary society which threaten and disrupt the institution of marriage. We will then reflect on the ways in which God breathes upon the family in order to sanctify it. Finally, we will probe the ways in which the Breath of God dispenses her charisms in order to transform family life into Christian ministry.

Marriage Under Siege.

Married life in this country is under siege from three different quarters. First, as individualism erodes the moral fabric of American society, it undermines people's capacity to remain faithful to a life-long, mutual commitment. Second, disillusionment with the Victorian family has brought the family itself into disrepute. Third, with the dwindling of the American middle class, parents find it harder and harder to make ends meet, even when both work full time. Let us reflect on each of these forces in turn.

Like other misleading moral attitudes, individualism distorts legitimate values into vice. Individualism roots itself in the true belief that every individual enjoys a sacred dignity, but individualism renders that belief vicious by exalting the value of the individual above that of society as a whole. Utilitarian individualists believe that society results from a contract among individuals bent on advancing their private interests. As a consequence, they feel bound by no social constraints that encroach upon personal self-interest. Expressive individualists believe that each person is endowed with a unique core of feeling and intuition which craves expression and that self-expression takes precedence over concern for the feelings and needs of others. Put simply,

to the archetypal imagination the breast from which we drink in that same divine wisdom.

Plants spring from Mother Earth; and the fruit of some plants can be used as intoxicants and hallucinogens. The archetype of the feminine accordingly associates the lady of the plants with visions and religious enlightenment. As we have seen, the Bible consistently attributes all forms of graced enlightenment to the Breath of God. She empowers us by her charisms, and she breathes the wisdom from on high. We call her enlightenment a prophetic anointing.

The archetype of the feminine connotes not only the conception but the transformation of life; and the Christian imagination has traditionally linked the Breath of God to rebirth unto eternal life.

Finally, women turn to men in love. The Breath of God gives herself to the Father by inspiring his creative and providential wisdom; and she conceives within God the Son, the Word of God who became flesh.

With their heads Christians perceive the Breath of God as a divine person, but to date they lack an image to relate to Her with their hearts. The human imagination has no sexless images of persons. If, then, we ever hope to supply for the lack of a personal image of God's Breath, we will have to imagine her as either male or female. Scripture, tradition, and the archetypal structure of the human psyche all sanction imagining her as feminine.

I have been trying to show that the archetype of the feminine in its positive, life-giving connotations has the capacity to connote all those impersonal images which the Christian imagination has traditionally associated with the Breath of God. The issue I am raising touches on a fundamental dimension of our relationship to God in faith. When Jesus changed the name of God to Papa he invited his followers to relate to God with new intimacy and trust. Christians relate to Jesus with an analogous intimacy when they call him brother and friend. The time has come to include the third person of the trinity in this circle of divine intimacy; and we can begin to do that by imagining her as Mama, as the one who conceives divine life in us and like a loving mother nurtures us to the fullness of risen life in Christ.

At a time when family life in this country gives serious signs of deteriorating, it might seem to some inopportune to imagine the triune God in familial images. As we have seen, divorce, sexual oppression within marriage, abortion, and child abuse have sinfully distorted many an American family.

No sinful distortions, however, mar the life of the divine family. Its members give themselves to one another with a totality of love that creates the identity of life they share from all eternity. When, therefore, we call the Breath of God the divine Mother and imagine the social life of the triune God in familial terms, we remind ourselves of the kind of love which ought to bond Christian families. We also remind ourselves that socialization into the divine family requires of us the willingness to treat all people as brothers and sisters; for the divine Mother broods over this broken world, healing the divisions and injustices that separate sinful humans from one another and gathering all people into the one family of God.

Appendix A: Theological Speculation on the Personal Character of the Holy Breath

This appendix originally appeared as the first part of Chapter V. Its somewhat technical character demoted it, however, to its present diminished status as an appendage to the final chapter. In it I attempt to summarize theological speculation on the personal character of the third person of the trinity. I include it here for those readers who would enjoy and profit from a more detailed account of this particular theological controversy.

I. Patristic Foundations.

The first Christians glorified the Father through the Son in His Breath. They experienced the divine Breath's illumination and testified to her empowering presence. They did not speculate extensively about her reality. Speculative insight into the Breath of God came later. In this respect a Christian understanding of the Holy Breath imitates the patterns of thought we find in the Old Testament. As we saw in the first chapter, the Hebrews knew the Breath of God through her prophetic inspirations but did not reflect on her reality until the writing prophets claimed the inspiration of God's word rather than of his Breath.

Although some New Testament writers speak of the saving action of the divine Breath in ways that suggest that they regarded her as a personal reality (Rom 8:14, 16, 26, Gal 4:6, 1 Cor 2:11; Acts 5:1-6; Jn 14:16-17, 26, 16:7-17), nowhere does the New Testament describe the Holy Breath of Jesus as a divine person. How, then, did Christians come to profess such a belief? In point of fact it took Christian theologians several centuries to explain what they meant by calling the Breath of God a divine person. It all began in the second century with a heresy called modalism; but the Christian attempt to understand the third person of the trinity continues today.

Second-century modalists sacrificed the trinity of the Christain God for the sake of preserving the divine unity. The modalists held for only one person in God, the Father, who, however, had revealed himself in two different modes in the course of human history, namely, as Son and as Breath. In the eastern church the modalists likened these modes of the Father's self-revelation to the masks *(prosopa)* which ancient actors wore instead of makeup. As a consequence, orthodox Christian thinkers in the east generally avoided using the term *prosopon* to designate the divine persons, since the term had modalist connotations.

Speculation in the Latin church, however, took a somewhat different turn. The Latin word *persona* translated the Greek word *prosopon.* It too signified in Latin the masks actors wore. Nevertheless, in struggling against modalism, Tertullian, one of the most influential of the early Latin fathers (ca. 160-ca. 220), did not hesitate to apply the term "*persona* (person)" to designate the distinctive reality of Father, Son, and Breath (*Against Praxeas,* VIII). As a consequence, Latin Christians learned very early to speak of three divine persons in God. By the term "person" Tertullian seems to have meant, not a mask, but a communicating subject. He held in other words that Christians commune differently with each of the divine persons.

In the east, theologians developed a somewhat different way of talking about the distinct reality of Father, Son, and Breath. In the fourth century, Arius, a priest of Alexandria, raised a storm of controversy by denying the divinity of both the Son and the Breath. In 325 A.D. the Council of Nicea condemned Arian doctrine for denying that the Son is "one in being *(homoousios)*" with the Father; and in 381 A.D., after fifty-six years of bitter controversy, the Council of Constantinople vindicated the divinity of the divine Breath as well (DS 125-126, 150).

The Arian controversy forced the Greek fathers to begin to fashion a technical language for talking about the unity and trinity of God. They used "*ousia* (being)" to designate the divine reality common to Father, Son, and Breath and "*hypostasis* (entity)" to designate the particularity of each of the members of the divine triad. Still, the meaning of the term *"hypostasis"* remained vague in the writings of the Greek fathers. Basil of Caesarea, for example, described the divine persons as "modes of ineffable existence" (*On the Holy Spirit,* 46).

When, however, the Arian controversy spread to the Latin church, the Latin fathers, following Tertullian's lead, translated the Greek term *"ousia"* by the Latin term "*substantia* (substance)" and the Greek term "*hypostasis* (entity)" by the Latin term "*persona* (person)." As a consequence, the Latin church in responding to the Arians defended the position that in the Christian God we find a single divine substance but three divine persons.

What, however, did the term "person" mean? Augustine of Hippo (354-430 A.D.) began to endow the term with some conceptual content when in his treatise on the trinity he linked the term person to relationship. He portrayed the divine persons as three subsisting relational realities in the Christian God. (*On the Trinity,* V, v, 1-xiv, 17).

II. Medieval Development.

Ancius Manlius Severinus Boethius, who flourished at the end of the fifth and the beginning of the sixth century, (ca. 474-524), formulated the first theological definition of the term "person." He did so in a short essay on the incarnation. Boethius defined a person as "the individual substance of a rational nature *(naturae rationabilis individua substantia)*" (*Contra Eutychen,* III, 1-5). After Boethius we find Christian thinkers agreeing that intelligence and particularity help define persons as persons.

In the twelfth century, however, Richard of St. Victor (d. 1173) in the course of criticizing Boethius' definition of the term "person" advanced theological insight into the reality of personal existence. As we have seen, Christian theologians in the west used the term "substance" to designate the divinity common to Father, Son, and Breath. Richard saw clearly and correctly that, if with Boethius one defines the three members of the trinity as intelligent, particular substances, one would be led logically to assert the presence of four substances in God: the one common to the three persons and the persons themselves. On the other hand, if one posited three distinct substances in God, one could seem to suggest that the Father, Son, and Breath are really three distinct gods (*De Trinitate,* IV, vi). Moreover, Richard argued if the divine persons differ as substances, they would have to differ the way that substances differ, namely, qualitatively (*De Trinitate,* IV, xiii-xv). If so, however, how could all three divine persons possess the same divinity? Since Richard found all of these suggestions unacceptable, he undertook to revise Boethius' definition of the term "person."

Richard described the divine persons as three "someones *(aliquos)* " who all possess the same divine substance and therefore share equally in the divine nature (*De Trinitate,* I xi). Instead of calling Father, Son, and Breath particular substances, however, Richard called them three different "existences *(existentiae).*" The term "existence" sounds pretty abstract but it had some interesting connotations for

Richard. First, it called attention to the relational character of the divine persons, to the fact that they derive their existence from one another. [The Latin word *"existentia"* is derived from the verb "subsist *(sistere)*" and the preposition "from *(ex).*"] Second, to Richard's mind the term "existence" did not connote qualitative difference in the way that the term "substance" does and therefore did not call into question the unity of the trinity. Finally and most important, the term "existence" connoted for Richard the ecstatic, social character of persons (*De Trinitate,* IV, x). This last insight has important implications for understanding the full reality of personal existence.

Richard of St. Victor understood the relationship of the divine persons to one another on an analogy with human personal existence. As the supreme exemplification of all that is good and beautiful, the divine persons delight in sharing the divine goodness with one another. They subsist eternally in a loving communion, a communion that resembles the love humans share even as it transcends mere human love utterly and completely (*De Trinitate,* III, ii-vi).

Richard, moreover, extended Boethius' thought on another important point: he regarded persons as particular, as so particular indeed that Richard denied that the divine persons could communicate the particular uniqueness each enjoyed to one another (*De Trinitate,* IV, xvi-xvii). Richard, therefore, defined a divine person as "an incommunicable existence of the divine nature" (*De Trinitate,* IV, xxi).

III. The Contemporary Debate

In the fourteenth century the English theologian John Duns Scotus (ca. 1265-1308) endorsed Richard's definition of a divine person (*In Librum Sententiarum,* 3, d. 1, q. 1, n. 10); and in the twentieth century, Heribert Muehlen has attempted to embellish further the thought of both Richard and Scotus with insights derived from existential philosophy. Following the existential philosopher Martin Buber,

Muehlen discovered the divine persons sharing analogously the same kinds of interpersonal relationships as human persons do.

For Muehlen, interpersonal relationships involve both knowing and willing, both understanding and love. "I-Thou" relationships bind together individuals in the intimate gift of themselves to one another. "We" relations unite loving communities of persons. Within the trinity the Son and the Father share an intimate I-Thou relationship, a relationship revealed historically in Jesus' perception of God as Abba (Papa). The Holy Breath transforms the trinity into a "We," a communion of persons sharing the same divine life in love.[1]

The preceding thumbnail sketch of Christian speculation on the reality of the divine persons suggests that as the centuries advanced, Christian theologians reached a shared, cumulative insight into the meaning of personal existence. They realized first that persons live in communion with one another. Next Christian thinkers proclaimed that persons enjoy particularity, a uniqueness that makes them concretely who they are. Eventually, some of them began to regard that uniqueness as incommunicable. Uniqueness, however, does not isolate persons from one another; for one cannot enjoy personal existence without standing in relationship with other persons. Christian thinkers discovered in interpersonal relationships mutual understanding and love. Most recently, they have distinguished two different kinds of interpersonal relationships: "I-Thou" relations and "We" relations. Indeed, the history of thought testifies that speculative concern with persons arose historically out of the Christian attempt to understand how three divine persons could enjoy the same divine life and how one divine person could possess at one and the same time both divinity and humanity. Philosophical speculation about human personal existence came much later.

[1]Heribert Muehlen, *Der Heilige Geist as Person* (Münster: Westfalen, 1963), *Una Mystica Persona: Fine Person in Vielen Personen* (Munich: Verlag Ferdinand Schonigh, 1968).

Not all theologians, however. like to speak of three persons in one God. The Protestant theologian Karl Barth, for example, objects to applying the term "person" to the three members of the trinity. He concedes that Father, Son, and Breath should be understood as special, distinct, absolutely individual relational ways of existing. He argues, however, that when people in the twentieth century use the term "person," it connotes for them the idea "personality." Because Barth denies the presence of God of three divine personalities, he prefers to speak of three really distinct modes of existence in God.[2]

Karl Rahner, S.J., one of the most influential of modern Catholic theologians, espoused a similar position but for different reasons. Because Rahner conceived of God as both infinite and absolutely mysterious, he hesitated to apply the term "person" both to creatures and to God. As a consequence, Rahner preferred to leave the reality of Father, Son, and Breath shrouded in "the ineffable darkness of the holy mystery." Moreover, because he regarded a human person as a "free center of consciousness and free activity which disposes of itself and differentiates itself from others," he feared that if we call the members of the trinity persons, we would jeopardize the unity of God by placing in the Godhead three distinct free and autonomous centers of consciousness.[3]

[2]Karl Barth, *Church Dogmatics*, translated by T.H.L. Parker, W.B. Johnson, H. Knight, J.L.M. Haire (New York: Scribners, 1957) I-I, 403-418.

[3]Karl Rahner, *Foundations of Christian Faith*, translated by William Dych, S.J. (New York: Seabury, 1978) 71-75.

Appendix B: A List of Latin Citations

I have in the course of the preceding reflections had occasion to cite a number of official church documents. In most cases these documents were promulgated at Vatican II. Official church documents are written in Latin and derive their names from the first few words of their Latin text. For those who do not read Latin I have supplied either in a footnote or in the text the common English name given to the document cited. Since that identification accompanies only the first citation of the document in question, I append here a list of these Latin titles and their English equivalents as an aid for readers who might wish to refer to the documents in question in English but who may have forgotten the English title.

- *Ad gentes: Decree on the Church's Missionary Activity*
- *Apostolicam actuousitatem: Decree on the Apostolate of the Laity*
- *Divinum illud munus: Encyclical Letter of Pope Leo XIII on the Holy Spirit*
- *Dominum et vivicantem: Encyclical Letter of Pope John Paul II on the Holy Spirit in the Church and the World*
- *DS:* Henry Denzinger and Adolf Schoenmetzer, S.J., eds. *Enchiridion Symbolorum Definitionum et*

Declarationum de Rebus Fidei et Morum (New York: Herder, 1967, [Title: *A Handbook of Creeds, Definitions, and Declarations About Matters of Faith and Morals*]

- *Gaudium et spes: Pastoral Constitution on the Church in the Modern World*
- *Lumen gentium: Dogmatic Constitution on the Church*
- *Mystici corporis: Encyclical Letter of Pope Pius XII on the Mystical Body of Christ*
- *Presbyterorum ordinis: Decree on the Ministry and Life of Priests*

Appendix C: Suggestions for Further Reading

In writing this book I have not attempted to break new theological ground but to produce a teachable theological text that will provide a basis for reflection and discussion. As a consequence, the reader will find all the ideas in this book developed at greater length in other works. The following suggestions for further reading in no way exhaust the field of theological reflection on the Holy Breath; but they will help students flesh out the insights summarized in this book.

Exegetical Studies

George Montague's *The Holy Spirit: The Growth of a Biblical Tradition* (New York: Paulist, 1976) provides a text-by-text analysis of all the passages in the Bible that refer to the Breath of God. Eduard Schweizer's *The Holy Spirit,* translated by Reginald H. and Ilse Fuller (Philadelphia: Fortress, 1980) covers much the same ground somewhat differently and in less textual detail. John Koenig's, *Charismata: God's Gifts for God's People* (Philadelphia: Westminster, 1978) provides a lucid analysis of the New Testament witness to the Holy Breath's charismatic activity among the first Christians. James Dunn's *Jesus and the Spirit* (Philadelphia: Westminster, 1975) offers an excellent analysis of the Holy

Breath's inspiration of Jesus' vision and mission. In his analysis of her illumination of the Christian community, however, he interprets a charism somewhat arbitrarily as an occasional grace. For a pastoral reflection on important biblical insights into the Holy Breath's saving activity, see John Paul II, "Dominum et vivificantem," *Origins: NC Documentary Service,* (June 12, 1986), vol. 16, no. 4.

Historical Studies

Yves M.J. Congar's *I Believe in the Holy Spirit,* translated by David Smith (3 vols.; New York, Seabury, 1983) addresses a host of interrelated questions: the Christian experience of the Breath of God, the evolution of doctrinal teaching about her, her place in spirituality, contemporary theological discussions about her reality. Congar develops his argument from a fairly traditional Catholic viewpoint. He has, moreover, expanded his study with a fourth volume, *The Word and the Spirit,* translated by David Smith (San Francisco: Harper and Row, 1986). The fourth volume studies the ways in which the word and Breath of God conspire in building up the Christian community. Two other studies cover some of the same ground more briefly and from a Protestant perspective: Paul D. Opsahl (ed.), *The Holy Spirit in the Life of the Church* (Minneapolis: Augsberg, 1978) and Alasdair I.C. Heron, *The Holy Spirit: The Holy Spirit in the Bible, the History of Christian Thought, and Recent Theology* (Philadelphia: Westminster, 1983). An anthology by Hans Küng and Jürgen Moltmann, eds., *Conflicts about the Holy Spirit* (New York: Seabury, 1979) examines some of the major theological controversies about the Holy Breath from a contemporary ecumenical perspective.

Foundational Studies

Three of the books I have written approach the Christian experience of the Holy Breath from the standpoint of a technical theology of Christian conversion: *Experiencing God: A Theology of Human Emergence* (New York: Paulist, 1978), *Charism and Sacrament: A Theology of Christian Conversion* (London: S.P.C.K., 1976), and *The Divine Mother: A Trinitarian Theology of the Holy Spirit* (New York: University Press of America, 1984).

Studies of Contemporary Charismatic Piety

Leon Joseph Cardinal Suenens' *A New Pentecost?,* translated by Francis Martin (New York: Crossroad, 1974) provides a readable theological introduction to the Catholic charismatic renewal by a leading churchman. My own books *Pentecostalism: A Theological Viewpoint* (New York: Paulist, 1971) and *Pentecostal Piety* (New York: Paulist, 1972) also give a popular theological orientation to issues in contemporary charismatic piety.

Edward Malatesta, S.J., ed., *The Spirit of God in Christian Life* (New York: Paulist, 1977) collects together several more technical theological essays on the Breath's role in Christian spirituality. So too do: Edward D. O'Connor, C.S.C., *Perspectives on Charismatic Renewal* (Notre Dame: University of Notre Dame Press, 1975) and Kilian McDonnell, O.S.B., *The Holy Spirit and Power: The Catholic Charismatic Renewal* (New York: Doubleday, 1975). Kilian McDonnell's *The Charismatic Renewal and Ecumenism* (New York:-Paulist, 1978) studies the ecumenical implications of contemporary charismatic piety. All three of these anthologies view the charismatic renewal from a Catholic standpoint. Two technical ecumenical studies of contemporary charismatic piety which include voices from a variety of denominational perspectives have emerged from the Protestant Pentecostal tradition: Russell P. Spittler, ed., *Perspectives on the New Pentecostalism* (Grand Rapids: Baker Book House, 1976) and Cecil M. Robeck, Jr., ed. *Charismatic Experiences in History* (Peabody, Mass.: Hendrickson, 1985).

Lay Apostolate

Students who wish to explore more the responsibilities and charismatic inspiration of lay Christians should study, if they have not done so, the official church documents which deal with this question. I would recommend from the documents of Vatican II, *Lumen gentium* (Dogmatic Constitution on the Church), *Apostolicam actuositatem* (Decree on the Apostolate of the Laity), and *Gaudium et Spes* (Pastoral Constitution on the Church in the Modern World). The most recent pastorals of the North American bishops also deserve careful study and practical implementation: *The Challenge of Peace: God's Promise and Our Response* (National Conference of Catholic Bishops, 1983) and *Economic Justice for All* (National Conference of Catholic Bishops, 1987). Norbert F. Lofink's *Option for the Poor: The Basic Principles of Liberation Theology in the Light of the Bible* [translated by Linda M. Maloney (Berkeley, CA: Bibal Press, 1987)] lays biblical foundations for a preferential option for the poor in the matter of social reform. Paul Steidl-Meier's *Social Justice Ministry: Foundations and Concerns* (New York: Le Jacq, 1984) provides a rather comprehensive theological basis for Christian social activism which he derives especially from official church teaching. Arthur Simon's *Christian Faith and Public Policy: No Grounds for Divorce* (Grand Rapids, MI: Eerdmans 1987) argues eloquently for the moral inevitability of Christian commitment to institutional reform. For a thoughtful reflection on the challenges which life in a neo-capitalistic, consumer society poses to contemporary Christians, see: John Francis Kavanaugh, *Following Christ in A Consumer Society* (New York: Orbis, 1986).